Sirtfood Diet

A Simple Guide to Losing Weight, Burning Fat and Feeling Better, Includes a Meal Plan and 100+ Recipes

© Copyright 2021

The content contained within this book may not be reproduced, duplicated or transmitted without direct written permission from the author or the publisher.

Under no circumstances will any blame or legal responsibility be held against the publisher, or author, for any damages, reparation, or monetary loss due to the information contained within this book, either directly or indirectly.

Legal Notice:

This book is copyright protected. It is only for personal use. You cannot amend, distribute, sell, use, quote or paraphrase any part, or the content within this book, without the consent of the author or publisher.

Disclaimer Notice:

Please note the information contained within this document is for educational and entertainment purposes only. All effort has been executed to present accurate, up to date, reliable, complete information. No warranties of any kind are declared or implied. Readers acknowledge that the author is not engaging in the rendering of legal, financial, medical or professional advice. The content within this book has been derived from various sources. Please consult a licensed professional before attempting any techniques outlined in this book.

By reading this document, the reader agrees that under no circumstances is the author responsible for any losses, direct or indirect, that are incurred as a result of the use of information contained within this document, including, but not limited to, errors, omissions, or inaccuracies.

Contents

PART 1: SIRTFOOD DIET 1
INTRODUCTION 2
SECTION ONE: WHAT IS THE SIRTFOOD DIET? 3
CHAPTER 1: THE SIRTFOOD DIET 4
How Is Your Body Affected by the Sirtfood Diet? 6
Phases of the Sirtfood Diet 7
Benefits of the Sirtfood Diet 8
CHAPTER 2: THE SCIENCE OF SIRTUINS 9
How Does Sirtuins Work? 9
How Does the Presence of Sirtuins Affect Our Body? 10
The Seven Types of Sirtuins 11
The Impact of Dietary Compounds on Sirtuins 14
CHAPTER 3: THE BENEFITS OF SIRTUINS 17
CHAPTER 4: IS THE SIRTFOOD DIET FOR YOU? 22
SECTION TWO: FOLLOWING THE DIET 26
CHAPTER 5: TOP 20 SIRTFOODS 27
CHAPTER 6: PHASE 1: GETTING STARTED 38
Phase 1 Plan 38
Insights or Experiences after Phase 1 46
CHAPTER 7: PHASE 2: MAINTENANCE 49
Phase 2 of the Sirtfood Diet 49
Plan Your Meals 53
Add Sirtfoods as a Regular Part of Your Meals 53

CHAPTER 8: INCORPORATING EXERCISE 55
TYPES OF EXERCISES YOU CAN INCLUDE ON THE SIRTFOOD DIET 56
SECTION THREE: MEAL PLANNING AND RECIPES 64
CHAPTER 9: SHOPPING LIST 65
FRUITS AND VEGETABLES 65
HERBS AND SPICES 66
DAIRY PRODUCTS 66
CONDIMENTS 67
MEAT 67
MISCELLANEOUS 67
MAKING A BUDGET AND SAVING MONEY 69
TOOLS AND EQUIPMENT REQUIRED 72
CHAPTER 10: MEAL PLANNER 75
COMMON MISCONCEPTIONS 80
21-DAY SIRTFOOD DIET MEAL PLAN 83
CHAPTER 11: RECIPES 96
1. SIRTFOOD GREEN JUICE 97
2. WALNUT AND DATE PORRIDGE 99
3. EGG AND MUSHROOM SCRAMBLE 101
4. SIRTFOOD SALAD 103
5. PRAWN STIR-FRY WITH BUCKWHEAT NOODLES 105
6. STRAWBERRY BUCKWHEAT TABBOULEH 107
7. SIRTFOOD BLUEBERRY PANCAKES 109
8. TURMERIC, CHICKEN, AND KALE CURRY 111
9. BAKED SALMON AND MINT SALAD 113
10. SIRTFOOD SHAKSHUKA 115
11. DARK CHOCOLATE GRANOLA BARS 117
12. CHICKEN SKEWERS WITH SATAY SAUCE 119
13. SIRTFOOD BITES 122
14. SIRTFOOD CHICKPEA STEW WITH BAKED POTATOES 124
15. KALE AND RED ONION DHAL WITH BUCKWHEAT 126
CONCLUSION 128
PART 2: SIRTFOOD RECIPES 130

A COOKBOOK WITH 100+ RECIPES FOR MAKING THE MOST OF THE SIRTFOOD DIET 130

   INTRODUCTION 131

   SECTION ONE: SIRTFOOD DIET BASICS 133

   CHAPTER 1: WHAT IS THE SIRTFOOD DIET? 134

      SIRTUIN FOODS 136

   CHAPTER 2: HOW TO FOLLOW THE SIRTFOOD DIET 137

      PHASE 1 137

      PHASE 2 138

   SECTION TWO: SIRTFOOD RECIPES 139

   CHAPTER 3: BEVERAGES 140

      GREEN JUICE #1 140

      GREEN JUICE # 2 141

      GREEN JUICE # 3 141

      KALE AND CELERY JUICE 142

      PARSLEY JUICE WITH GINGER AND APPLE 142

      STRAWBERRY SMOOTHIE 145

      MIXED BERRY SMOOTHIE 146

      CHOCOLATE SMOOTHIE 146

      APPLE PIE SMOOTHIE 147

      BLUEBERRY PIE SMOOTHIE 148

      BERRY & GREEN TEA SMOOTHIE 148

      MATCHA GREEN TEA AND PINEAPPLE SMOOTHIE 149

      ORANGE AND MANGO GREEN TEA SMOOTHIE 150

      PARSLEY, PINEAPPLE, AND BANANA SMOOTHIE 150

      COCONUT OIL LATTE 151

      Matcha Latte *151*

      GOLDEN TURMERIC LATTE 152

      COCONUT OIL HOT CHOCOLATE 153

      PEACH GREEN ICED TEA 153

   CHAPTER 4: BREAKFAST 155

      GREEN GODDESS SCRAMBLED EGGS 155

      MUSHROOM SCRAMBLED EGGS 156

Tofu Scramble with Kale and Sweet Potatoes 157
Blueberry Banana Pancakes with Chunky Apple Compote 158
Strawberry Chocolate Chip Buckwheat Pancakes 159
Apple Pancakes with Blackcurrant Compote 161
Chocolate Cream Pancake 162
Shakshuka 163
Date and Walnut Porridge 164
Healthy Matcha Green Tea Overnight Oats 165
Choco-Chip Granola 166
Smoked Salmon Omelet 167
Buckwheat Superfood Muesli 167
Grain Bowl 168
Buckwheat and Eggs 169
Savory Tempeh Breakfast Sandwich 169

CHAPTER 5: SOUPS 171
Greens and Grains Soup 171
Winter Vegetable Soup with Butternut Squash & Cauliflower 172
Beans and Farro Soup 173
Broccoli and Kale Green Soup 174
Miso Ramen Soup with Buckwheat Noodles 176
Strawberry Melon Soup with Mint 177
Vegetarian Pasta Soup 178
Caldo de Res (Mexican Beef Soup) 179
Cioppino 181
Bitter Greens with Cheese Dumplings Soup 182
Lovage, Lettuce, Pea and Cucumber Soup 184

CHAPTER 6: LUNCH RECIPES 185
Salmon Super Salad 185
Green Juice Salad 186
Broccoli, Edamame & Cabbage Millet Salad 187
Salmon Pasta Salad with Lemon & Capers 188
California Kale Cobb Salad 189

Fresh Fruit and Kale Salad 190
Warm Chicory Salad with Mushrooms.. 191
Courgette and Lovage Pasta.. 192
Strawberry Buckwheat Tabbouleh 193
Spring Vegetable & Cauliflower Tabbouleh 194
Buckwheat Crepes 195
Buckwheat Stir Fry with Kale, Peppers & Artichokes 196
Chicken and Kale Curry 197
Crispy Turmeric Roasted Potatoes 199
Buckwheat Pancakes 200
Kale And Feta Frittata 201
Parsley Detox Wrap 202
Roast Beef Wrap 202
Chickpea, Quinoa and Turmeric Curry 203

CHAPTER 7: SNACKS 205

Buckwheat Granola 205
Chocolate Coconut Vegan Energy Balls 206
Healthy Matcha Green Tea Fudge Bars 207
Sirtfood Bites 208
Dark Chocolate Cherry Energy Bites 209
Sunflower-Coated Cheesy Kale Chips 210

QUINOA & KALE MUFFINS 212

Coffee Gelatin and Mascarpone Cheese 213
Key Lime Coconut Energy Bites 214
Herbed Cheese Ball 215
Vegan Tofu "Fish" Sticks 216
No-Bake Rawies 217
Tomato Bruschetta 217
Strawberry and Coconut Ice-Blocks 218
Berry Smoothie Ice-Blocks 219
Superfood Trail Mix 219

CHAPTER 8: VEGETARIAN 221

Vegetable Omelet 221

Kale Stir Fry with Crispy Curried Tofu 222
Kale, Pumpkin Seed and Potato One Pot Dinner 223
Springtime Buckwheat Risotto 224
Miso & Sesame Glazed Tofu Stir-Fry 226
Veggie Sandwich 227
Ricotta Sandwiches with Carrots, Kale and Walnut-Parsley Pesto 228
Squash and Kale Gratin Casserole 230
Three-Bean Chili with Spring Pesto 231
Apple Glazed Vegetable & Edamame Stir-Fry 232
Kale, Edamame and Tofu Curry 233
Shirataki Noodles with Kale and Chickpeas 234

CHAPTER 9: DINNER **236**
Spiced Cauliflower Couscous with Chicken 236
Chicken Noodles 237
Aromatic Chicken Breast with Kale, Red Onion and Salsa 238
Chicken Marsala *240*
Chicken Skewers with Satay Sauce 242
Turkey Apple Burgers 244
Turkey Sandwiches with Apple and Walnut Mayo *245*
Sautéed Turkey with Tomatoes and Cilantro 246
Steak with Spicy Chimichurri Sauce 247
Chargrilled Beef with Red Wine Jus, Onion Rings, Garlic Kale and Herb Roasted Potatoes 248
Orecchiette with Sausage and Chicory 249
Chili Con Carne 250
Lamb, Butternut Squash and Date Tagine 252
Lamb and Black Bean Chili 253
Tomato, Bacon and Arugula Quiche with Sweet Potato Crust 254
Lentil and Sausage Stew 256
Chinese-Style Tofu and Pork with Bok Choy 257
Turmeric Baked Salmon 258
Asian King Prawn Stir-Fry with Buckwheat Noodles 260

Walnut and Dijon Crusted Halibut 261
Greek Salmon 262
Fresh Saag Paneer 264
Asian Hot Pot 265
Quinoa Kale Pesto Bowl with Poached Eggs 266
Braised Puy Lentils 268
Baked Potatoes with Spicy Chickpea Stew 269
Kale and Red Onion Dhal with Buckwheat 270
Tuscan Bean Stew 271
Wine & Grilled Cheese 272
Red Wine Roasted Mushrooms on Goat Cheese Garlic Toasts 273
Kale & Garlic Frittata 274

CHAPTER 10: DESSERTS **276**
Chocolate Cupcakes with Matcha Icing 276
Healthy Matcha Cake with Matcha Frosting 278
Buckwheat Chocolate Walnut Brownie *280*
Healthy Matcha Green Tea Coconut Fudge 281
Vegan Buckwheat Chocolate Chip Cookies 282
Buckwheat Double Chocolate Cookies 283
Healthy Matcha Green Tea Ice Cream 284
Coffee Ice Cream 285
Dark Chocolate Mousse 287
Blueberry Cobbler 288

SPICED RED WINE-POACHED PEARS **288**
Date Squares 289
Strawberry Rhubarb Crunch 291

SECTION THREE: MEAL PLANNING **292**
CHAPTER 11: WHY MEAL PLANNING IS IMPORTANT **293**
What is Meal Planning? 293
Benefits of Meal Planning 294

CHAPTER 12: YOUR SIRTFOOD MEAL PLAN **295**
Sample Sirtfood Diet Meal Plan 295

Week One *295*
Week Two *297*
Week Three *298*
Week Four *299*
CONCLUSION 301
RESOURCES 303
REFERENCES 304

Part 1: Sirtfood Diet

How You Can Lose Weight, Burn Fat and Feel Better Overall While Following a Simple Meal Plan Filled with Delicious Recipes

Introduction

Would you believe it if someone told you that you could lose around 5 to 7 lbs. a week while consuming coffee, wine, and chocolate? It seems too good to be true, doesn't it? Well, it isn't! A new diet, known as the Sirtfood Diet, is revolutionizing the world of health and fitness, especially after well-known celebrities have lost excessive amounts weight by following this outline.

The Sirtfood Diet has become wildly popular because of its impressive success rate. If you have tried other diets, such as Keto, Paleo, and intermittent fasting, and you still struggle to lose weight, it's time to give the Sirtfood Diet a shot.

The Sirtfood Diet is now known as "the diet that allows wine and chocolate." Yes, it's true, but before you jump on the bandwagon, learn how it works, the science behind it, and the food you'll be able to eat so you can follow it safely.

If you are new to the Sirtfood Diet and want to learn more about it, you've come to the right place. This book is a comprehensive guide that will teach you everything about the Sirtfood Diet – how it works, the benefits, popular sirt foods, how to get started, how to lose the pounds, and how to maintain the new weight. It includes easy recipes you can make at home every day and provides the latest expert insights that will boost your chances of losing weight and help speed up your weight loss journey.

Are you excited? Let's get started.

SECTION ONE: What is the Sirtfood Diet?

Understanding the theoretical and scientific aspects of the Sirtfood Diet will help you determine whether this new lifestyle is right for you. In the following chapters, you will gain in-depth knowledge about sirtuins and how these work in your body to support you in losing weight. Let's take a look.

Chapter 1: The Sirtfood Diet

Before we discuss popular sirtfoods and meal plans, it is essential to understand this nutrition plan's mechanism, that is far more complex than consuming fewer calories than you burn. Sirtfoods include "sirtuins," which are proteins known for protecting the body cells against inflammation, stress, and aging.

Helped by the Sirtfood Diet, many celebrities and notable figures swear by this way of eating. Even though it was discovered in 2016, the world became more aware recently. It was developed by health experts Aidan Goggins and Glen Matten, who focus on healthy eating. The idea is to turn on your "skinny gene" which means activating the sirtuin compounds discovered in your body to boost metabolism, reduce inflammation, cut fat, curb appetite, and lose weight.

Sirtuins are one of the many protein groups naturally created in the body, like hemoglobin. Although they don't directly cause weight loss, they regulate cellular health. One of the side effects of being activated through certain food groups is consistent weight loss until the individual in question reaches a healthy weight. Contrary to popular belief, they are not a type of dietary protein.

Sirtuins were discovered no more than 20 years ago, so it's safe to say that the Sirtfood Diet is still in the experimental phase. Although, there is plenty of anecdotal evidence that confirms the efficacy of the plan.

A simple way to understand how this group works is to think of it as part of a system with different departments – those being protein groups. Hemoglobin is a department that transports oxygen to cells; sirtuins are another branch that removes acetyl groups from proteins with a compound known as nicotinamide adenine dinucleotide, or simply NAD+. We can think of it as the currency sirtuins need to function. Because NAD+ levels decline with age, this also helps to maintain those levels. As a result, the dieter benefits from glowing skin and a fitter body. The process is also identified as deacetylation, seeing as sirtuins primarily work to remove acetyl groups such as histones responsible for leaving the chromatin of body cells open and thus vulnerable. When histones are not removed, they can cause weight gain and premature aging. This is where the Sirtfood Diet comes to the rescue.

Goggins and Matten conducted a study in 2015 on 39 participants and the effect of sirtuins on individual bodies. They discovered that on average, all people lost seven pounds in a week. This claim was based on a short-term investigation partly due to introducing calorie restriction.

While the primary aim of this way of eating is to lose weight through healthy choices, the effect is maximized by introducing sirtuin-activating foods into your meals. In the presence of sirtuins, you will lose weight and benefit from anti-aging effects and the reduction of inflammation levels in your body.

How Is Your Body Affected by the Sirtfood Diet?

Sirtfood demands a major calorie restriction in the first week (with a caloric limit of 1,000 calories) and focuses on healthy eating. Experts recommend this as a long-term fitness plan (even though it's difficult to maintain) as it focuses more on following a healthy lifestyle and less on weight loss. Once you follow this diet for a few weeks, you will lose weight and become fitter, but since it restricts calories in the first week, dieters can experience a massive drop on the scale in the first week. The difference in body weight is mainly due to water loss, not actual loss of body fat.

You will notice a remarkable change in your body weight by the end of the first week because the glycogen molecules extracted from the food you eat usually require around three to four molecules of water as storage. We need glycogen to carry out day-to-day bodily functions and meet physical and mental energy needs. When on a calorie-restricted plan, the body uses up all maximum glycogen along with the water it stores, which significantly reduces water content, ultimately shedding a massive amount of water weight. This is why you will notice a difference on the scale after just one week of beginning the Sirtfood Diet.

When you return to a diet plan with a regular caloric intake, the glycogen molecules in your body retain the water particles, and you will notice your weight returning to normal. A low-calorie diet results in a lower metabolic rate, resulting in weight loss and the burning of body fat. To successfully shed weight, distribute your meals throughout the day. As soon as you eat, your body's metabolic rate increases and burns calories; This is why you may feel warm after eating. Another way to increase your metabolic rate is to incorporate exercise to your every-day routine. The metabolic rate of your body thus increases for a prolonged period after your workout session.

Since your body is on a major calorie restriction for the first couple of weeks, refrain from exercising as it can put too much stress on your body. If you already work out and don't want to go back to square one, you can still incorporate mild exercises like walking and yoga.

Phases of the Sirtfood Diet

The Sirtfood Diet is divided into two phases:

Phase 1: This lasts for the first seven days of your daily routine and requires you to eat 1,000 calories in a day. These calories are distributed throughout the day and consumed through three glasses of green juice and one main sirtfood meal (keep reading to learn more about green juices, sirtfood meals and how to make them). The next four days, you may consume 1,500 calories throughout the day, including two green juices and two sirtfood meals. During this phase, you lose around five to ten pounds within seven days, which is mostly your water weight. You may notice that your face is more sculpted and your belly is less bloated. The success of Phase 1 determines the end results, which can be achieved within the two weeks.

Phase 2: The second phase focuses more on maintaining your weight loss and is carried out over the following 14 days. Once you endure the first week, which is also the most difficult and important phase, you can switch to three sirtfood meals and one green juice a day. You'll continue to consume the same types of ingredients, sirtfoods, and a glass of green juice over the next 14 days. You must maintain the calorie and nutrient count over these two weeks; this is why it is called the "maintenance phase". If followed consistently, you can maintain weight loss during this time and turn your new diet into a permanent, healthy way of eating.

Since this diet's main goal is to incorporate healthy eating into your lifestyle, it follows a 21-day dieting approach. It takes only 21 days to turn into a habit perfectly, which is why the first step to incorporating this diet for the long term is to follow the 21-day plan without a single cheat meal. By the 22nd day, you will crave sirtfoods and you will not feel as restricted.

Luckily, even if you get sidetracked for a while, you can always start over. Even though the diet is calorie-restricted, the interesting meals included will keep you hooked. Typical recipes such as chicken skewers, pancakes, and pizza can all be consumed on this diet, as long as your calorie intake is in check. The easiest way to keep eating you love to replace common ingredients with sirtfoods.

Benefits of the Sirtfood Diet

- While weight loss is the most noticeable benefit, several other positive effects are associated with this diet.

- Slows down the aging process and can help prevent the appearance of wrinkles and fine lines.

- Reduces inflammation.

- Detoxifies the body and helps ward off various diseases.

- Can help sustain your health for a longer period.

- Supports and promotes longevity.

The Sirtfood Diet has recently caused a whirlwind of excitement around the world, and rightly so. It's effective, and the immediate results dieters get are what keeps them hooked. You, too, can begin your journey by restocking your pantry and planning your meals.

Chapter 2: The Science of Sirtuins

In this chapter, we will delve into the details about sirtuins and the science behind them. Beginning with describing what sirtuins are, and how they work, followed by the science behind these compounds.

How Does Sirtuins Work?

In the Sirtfood Diet, you may eat healthy foods, such as kale and strawberries. This diet allows almost every type of fruit, vegetable, or food item rich in polyphenols. Since polyphenols activate the sirtuins protein in your body, the Sirtfood Diet is built around similar foods. When the polyphenol compounds activate these sirtuins, your body undergoes changes that mimic the effect of exercising and fasting. Ultimately, this helps you lose weight. Hence, it is necessary to load up on those options that contain polyphenols.

Sirtuins are also known as SIRTs, or silent information regulators, which affect your metabolic rate and hinder the aging process. Moreover, SIRTs also regulate the way sugar is broken down by your body to produce energy and store fat. This phenomenon is particularly necessary when your body undergoes major calorie restriction, which happens when you introduce sirtfoods in your diet. Since you burn more energy and store less fat, you ultimately lose weight.

Since the Sirtfood Diet is based on a calorie restriction method, sirtfoods aren't the only reason that fat gets cut. Even if you decrease calories on a normal diet, you will lose weight. It's mainly about calorie restriction and healthy eating, but the Sirtfood Diet takes a half and half approach - a calorie restriction paired up with the effect of sirtfoods. Due to this, the Sirtfood Diet is believed to be one of the most effective calorie-restricted diets that help lose weight in a jiffy. The Sirtfood Diet activates SIRTs in the mitochondria of every cell in your body, thus helping you lose weight, the low calorie-diet also helps you steer clear from empty carbs, which contribute to the aging of your skin and body.

Now that you know what sirtuins are, also know the science behind these molecules.

How Does the Presence of Sirtuins Affect Our Body?

All mammals and humans have seven different types of sirtuins in their body cells' mitochondria, which are SIRT-1 through SIRT-7. These seven types of SIRTs carry out unique functions but collectively work to maintain the longevity of your body and halt the aging process. Although preventing premature aging can be done by reducing calorie intake, sirtuin-activating foods affect the efficacy of sirtuins in your body on a much bigger scale.

Reducing your calorie intake affects the way they work, or *enhances* the activity, making them more efficient in slowing down aging, preventing inflammation and combating the negative side effects of stress. This also comes with several other health benefits.

The initial research on sirtuins, which was conducted at MIT, can be dated to 1991. One of the first sirtuins discovered was found in Saccharomyces cerevisiae, a species of yeast, also known as baker's yeast. This sirtuin was named Sir2 - Silent Information Regulator. The study also found that this sirtuin specifically enhanced the telomere length of human chromosomes and thus significantly slowed down the aging process.

Telomeres, found in every human cell, are the protective "caps" or ends of the chromosomes. As we grow older, our telomere length is compromised, and our bodies age, evidenced by weight gain, slow metabolism, and sagging of the skin. Recent studies over the last twenty years showed that telomere length was enhanced with higher sirtuin activity. Besides this, the SIRT levels detected in the study were also found to increase lifespan and decrease aging.

Since the structure is highly conserved, studies have not yet concluded the exact behavior and effect of them in human and animal bodies. Their presence in the animal kingdom can be dated to ancient times, so we know that they are not an evolutionary anomaly in humans.

The Seven Types of Sirtuins

Let's take a look at the seven types of sirtuins and how these affect your body.

SIRT-1: Ever since we discovered sirtuins as a protein group, SIRT-1 has been an element of curiosity. It was studied for many years and was the primary component of research in most longevity case studies. Calorie restriction supports the positive response of this particular sirtuin in promoting anti-aging and other related health advances. The up-regulation with calorie restriction was also concluded to offer neurological health benefits and support. Besides this, SIRT-1 is also known to induce homologous recombination within human cells, promoting DNA repair and recombining the breaks that occur in DNA, supporting healthy body cells and longevity. It is also particularly useful in combating inflammation and boosting metabolism.

Besides this, this sirtuin type protects the human body from metabolic diseases, induces a stress response, and prevents cardiovascular conditions and various cancers. Last, it is also known to affect the body's neurological responses and protects it from several neurodegenerative disorders.

SIRT-2: This protein is notably useful for people struggling with extra fat, particularly obese individuals. When paired with calorie restriction, this sirtuin breaks excess fat tissue, helping them reach a healthy weight through rapid fat loss. But it increases fat tissue in animals. Mainly found in the cytoplasm and partly in the nucleus, SIRT-2 promotes cell growth and protects the degeneration of old cells. Although, we need more studies and research to understand the pathological and physiological functions of this protein. The main functions of this protein include tumorigenesis and cell expansion.

SIRT-3: This sirtuin is probably the most effective in terms of antioxidant properties. Low levels of this sirtuin in animals can activate the effect of free radicals, which can cause oxidative damage. If your body has high levels of free radicals, it can be difficult for you to lose weight. The main purpose of SIRT-3 is to boost metabolism and induce weight loss.

Collectively, SIRT-1, SIRT-2, and SIRT-3 promote numerous health benefits, such as:

- Burning excess fat and preventing further accumulation
- Inducing the release of insulin and controlling blood sugar levels.
- Regulating beta cells in the pancreas are regulated, which controls insulin levels.
- Reducing the production of glucose in the liver and reduces the chances of fat accumulation and obesity.
- Promoting the growth of muscle cells by encouraging the advancement of new mitochondria.

- Discouraging fat formation and growth, or adipogenesis.

- Continuously supporting the production of HDL cholesterol, otherwise known as the healthy kind.

- Training the muscles to react to insulin sensitivity, which improves glucose absorption in the blood streamline.

- Allowing the fat cells to receive more adiponectin, which stimulates a widened inflammatory response.

SIRT-4: As mentioned previously, chromosomes consist of end caps known as telomeres that preserve their life and structure. Without these, they deteriorate and shorten with age. For this reason, the presence of SIRT-4 is necessary. This protein increases insulin secretion, which regulates blood sugar levels and protects the body from related diseases such as diabetes. SIRT-4 is directly related to insulin sensitivity and helps to regulate it.

SIRT-5: This protein type is mainly responsible for ammonia detoxification by converting ammonia to urea. In the process of combating free radicals and harmful toxins, this conversion takes place and urea is excreted through urination. SIRT-5 regulates the functions of detoxification in the human body, which prepares it for weight loss.

SIRT-6: This type is believed to be the most effective in increasing longevity. More research will be required for this claim to be proven. Similar to SIRT-1, this sirtuin helps repair damaged DNA and DNA breaks. It is a protein bound to chromatin, which removes acetyl groups from the amino acids found in the foods we consume – an essential process to detoxification and DNA renewal.

Besides this, if SIRT-6 is present in excess, it can cause homologous recombinational repair. In recent studies, it was shown that the absence of SIRT-6 in animals could lead to several aging issues even in the early years of life. Signs of low SIRT-6 activities include bone degeneration, immune deficiency, and colitis.

Further, SIRT-6 also assists in secreting an enzyme called cytokine, a tumor necrosis factor (TNF), which fights systemic inflammation and helps prevent certain forms of cancer. It can also boost metabolism and repair DNA.

SIRT-7: This protein is known for its non-homologous end-joining properties that correct double-strand breaks of DNA. In several studies conducted on mice, it was found this protein prevented premature aging and reduced the aging of cells. Although, SIRT-7 is mainly responsible for RNA transcription.

The seven types exist in different components within cells of human bodies. For instance, SIRT-2 is found in cytoplasm, SIRT-1, SIRT-6, and SIRT-7 are found in the nucleus, while SIRT-3, SIRT-4, and SIRT-5 are found in the mitochondria.

Even though the studies are still in progress, and we need more substantial evidence to support these claims, it is definite that several natural substances affect the functioning of sirtuins and improve results. For instance, these components in human bodies, such as hormones, nutrients, and botanical extracts, affect sirtuins in some way or another. Further claims on the effects of other natural materials over sirtuins can be proven only after a thorough animal and test-tube study.

The Impact of Dietary Compounds on Sirtuins

Different components in your body react differently to SIRTs and produce varied effects. These components can be hormones, nutrients, or even botanical extracts.

Let's take a look at these compounds and how these effects in the body.

1. Pterostilbene

This antioxidant component, which is abundantly found in blueberries, stimulates SIRT-1, which promotes anti-inflammatory properties. Pterostilbene up-regulates and stimulates SIRT-1, which targets the body parts affected by inflammation and reduces free-radicals' negative effect. Besides this, pterostilbene also encourages more oxygen flow to our heart, which stimulates cell renewal and protection.

2. NAD

NAD, or Nicotinamide Adenine Dinucleotide, is a chemical compound naturally found in the body. It's known to be a major contributing factor to boosting metabolism. There are 2 types of NAD-, NAD+, and NADH. High NAD+ levels are needed for sirtuins to function, while the human bodies also need NR or Nicotinamide riboside to sustain NAD+ levels. Once the NR levels are increased in your body, NAD+ levels increase, too. This up-regulates and encourages the function of sirtuins in the body, where the benefits of anti-aging, anti-inflammation, and detoxification are reaped. NR levels can be affected by calorie restriction.

3. Resveratrol

This compound is commonly found in red wine and up-regulates and stimulates various sirtuins and promotes many health benefits. SIRT-1 is the most affected and up-regulated by this compound, promoting anti-aging and DNA renewal. This is why it's presumed that drinking a glass of red wine sometimes can prevent fine lines and wrinkles on your skin. Further, it is also known to stimulate the sirtuin's antioxidant properties that help fight free radicals and flushes out toxins. Resveratrol is also believed to enhance insulin resistance, which regulates blood sugar levels. SIRT-4 is also affected by this compound, which helps protect telomeres from being damaged by free radicals.

4. Melatonin

Abundantly found in eggs, fish and nuts, melatonin boosts the activity of sirtuins in general. Although, the main sirtuin this compound stimulates is SIRT-1. Melatonin is commonly known as a sleep aid, and it is naturally found in the body at night, signaling the body that it's time to rest, but supplements are not recommended, especially if you take anti-depressants because they can reduce dopamine levels.

5. Curcumin

Curcumin is frequently found in turmeric and acts as a flavonoid which is a group of plant-based compounds known to have antioxidant properties. Other flavonoids are typically found in fruits, vegetables, herbs, and spices.

Similar to other compounds, curcumin up-regulates SIRT-1 significantly, which offers antioxidant properties and protects the nervous system by supporting nerve cell growth and preventing nerve damage. Besides SIRT-1, curcumin up-regulates SIRT-3, SIRT-5, SIRT-6, and SIRT-7. Overall, the compound protects the nervous system, boosts immunity, and detoxifies the body.

All in all, they are believed to enhance bodily functions and promote several health benefits. It is why we need a sirtfood-rich diet low in calories.

Chapter 3: The Benefits of Sirtuins

Now that you know what sirtuins are and how they work, let's delve into their benefits and why your diet needs to include sirtuin-activating foods.

As previously explained, sirtuins offer several benefits besides aiding weight loss. They help reduce inflammation, boost metabolism, curb appetite, and assist in detoxification. Let's take a look at each benefit in detail.

1. Reduce Inflammation

Inflammation is one of the major causes of bloating and an overall bulky appearance, and it has also been proven to lead to weight gain. If you want to lose weight, one of the factors that need to be focused on is your body's inflammation levels. SIRT-1 is the main sirtuin that prevents inflammation and controls various stress responses, including genotoxic stress, hypoxic stress, and heat shock. Consuming sirtuin-activating foods can effectively combat this issue. The best sirtuin to reduce pain is SIRT-1. When paired with oxidative stress, chronic inflammation can induce insulin resistance, increasing the risk for type 2 diabetes.

Further, the effects of inflammation are partly associated with metabolic rate. Even if there is a slight change in sirtuin levels, this can significantly change physiologic processes. When NAD+ levels are altered in the body, this can significantly affect the circadian rhythm, which is directly related to the cyclical activation of 2 main sirtuin types associated with inflammatory properties: SIRT-1 and SIRT-6. Whenever the circadian rhythm changes, affecting inflammation in the body. Activating sirtuins in the body reduces both chronic and acute inflammation.

When resveratrol is introduced to the diet, it stimulates the function of SIRT-1, which reduces chronic inflammation; this is also the case with an increase in levels of NAD+, which boosts metabolism or rebalances it if it is too low. This phenomenon also rebalances homeostasis.

2. Boost Metabolism

With constant regulatory effects on the most important body parts, such as heart, brain, nerves, immune system, blood vessels, and metabolism, sirtuins' effect is multifold. Out of all these benefits, the effect of sirtuins on metabolic rate is the most noteworthy (with weight loss and fitness). As you may already know, metabolism speeds up to burn more calories whenever one eats. Those who have a higher metabolic rate tend to lose weight even during rest, which is known as the resting metabolic rate. The bigger the resting metabolic rate is, the more calories are burned without this person exerting energy. It's significant to note that SIRT-1 is the most effective sirtuin in boosting metabolic rate.

As you can see, a greater metabolic rate is necessary to keep burning more calories and to lose or maintain body weight. Although. not everyone is blessed with a fast metabolism. One would intermittently need to eat throughout the day to keep metabolism up and running; but usually this could cause an adverse effect if the person in questions consumes more calories than they burn. It's advised to eat smaller meal portions every 2 to 3 hours, or to exercise every day to keep burning calories even when the body is at rest.

Another way to up metabolic rate is to include sirtuin-activating food, or sirtfoods, in a low-calorie diet. By consuming these regularly, you keep your metabolic rate high throughout the day.

For example, one popular sirtfood is the bird's-eye chili, which is an ingredient rich in sirtuins. It also has another important component known as capsaicin, which gives it a spicy taste and increases body temperature. This compound works hand-in-hand with sirtuins to increase metabolic rate.

Regular sleep is also necessary to keep the metabolic rate in check. Added stress and lack of sleep wreak havoc on eating patterns, ultimately leading to weight gain. It is advised to get at least seven to eight hours of sleep every night. This will reduce stress and provide more energy for more efficient exercise, which will ultimately burn more calories and keep metabolism high. You see, it's all connected!

3. Curb Appetite

It's no surprise that being on a restrictive diet can be challenging since it's natural to be bombarded by unwanted cravings and a constant need to binge-eat, especially at the early stages of following the diet. A frequent habit of snacking can increase hunger levels, even when the body does not need nutrition. When someone eats out of boredom and not hunger, they usually satiate cravings with sugar and unnecessary calories, which can lead to rapid weight gain and premature ageing.

Consuming sirtfoods can partly reduce cravings, which in turn curb appetite in the long run. Certain sirtfoods, such as buckwheat and strawberries, are packed with fiber that keeps you satiated for a long time and help prevent hunger. Ultimately, this places you within your calorie count, and you lose weight rapidly. So, if you are looking to reduce your sugar cravings, sirtfoods are your go-to.

4. Aid in Detoxification

Eating sirtuin-activating food activates the process that helps cells flush out waste and toxins from your body. Detoxification of harmful waste and toxins prepares the body for weight loss and keeps health issues at bay. Certain types of sirtuins, such as SIRT-5, spurs anti-oxidation properties in the presence of some compounds. It actively fights free radicals and reduces oxidative stress in your body. This not only aids you in losing weight but also promotes other correlated health benefits, such as slow aging and a boost in metabolic rate.

We all know the primary benefits of exercising. It not only burns calories and protects your heart's health but also increases detoxification by combating the harmful free radicals in a human body. This phenomenon, through exercising, is encouraged further by the up-regulation of sirtuins and their positive impact on our health.

5. Reduce Aging

Sirtuins also reduce the aging process of your body cells. Since these compounds accelerate aging and reduce inflammation, they rejuvenate your dying cells and support the production of new cells.

The anti-aging properties of sirtuins are particularly seen in yeast types like Caenorhabditis elegans and Drosophila. And mitochondrial biogenesis, PGC-1alpha, is regulated by SIRT-1, which provides several health benefits, with slow aging being one of the primary benefits. Resveratrol, which is another SIRT-1 activator, also increases the mechanism of mitochondrial biogenesis.

Frequent exercise is known to up-regulate the activity of sirtuins, particularly SIRT-1. An active lifestyle promotes various health benefits, so naturally, it will also arouse the positive effects of sirtuins. Even a mild exercise routine can stimulate the activity of SIRT-1. The effect increases with the intensity of the exercise. Besides this, it is believed that the effects of exercise on one's body have other health benefits. For instance, busy adults are protected from age-related sarcopenia, or muscle wasting, due to the increase of sirtuin activity.

6. Reduce Age-Related Neurological Diseases

Besides reducing physical and physiological age-related issues, sirtuins also protect your brain from aging and reduce age-related neurological diseases. These include Alzheimer's, Wallerian degeneration, Huntington's, and Parkinson's disease. Phenomena such as axonal degeneration and cell death of dopaminergic neurons are some causes of these neurodegenerative diseases; this is where sirtuins step in. The positive effects of SIRT-1 protect the brain from atrophy. However, SIRT-1 not only protects from nerve damage but also promotes cell regeneration and, sometimes, is stipulated to reverse neurological diseases.

So, all in all, SIRT-1, which promotes the longevity of the human mitochondria, boosts overall anti-aging of the body and mind. Paired with calorie restriction, enhanced results can be achieved. These properties also help combat cardiovascular diseases, seeing as free radicals and ageing trigger them. When activated with the compound resveratrol, this sirtuin's effects enhance vascular functions in a person's body and protects against heart-related issues.

Chapter 4: Is the Sirtfood Diet for You?

While the Sirtfood Diet is highly recommended for people trying to lose weight and get fit, first decide whether it's meant for you or not. Restricting calories and basing nutritional plans on sirtfoods are not suggested for individuals with underlying health issues. This especially goes for individuals with dysfunctional thyroids, hormonal imbalances, and deficiencies. It's advised to consult with a physician before following any new restrictive eating plan. This is notably true of the Sirtfood Diet as it cuts out entire food groups and limits calorie intake to 1000 calories for all individuals, regardless of their weight and height, which may exacerbate existing health complications for those with more demanding physiques or more active lifestyles.

If you're wondering if this way of eating is right for you, consider these questions.

1. Is Your Day or Routine Highly Active?

Since the Sirtfood Diet cuts back on calories on a massive scale, it shouldn't be followed by individuals who are highly active during the day. Calorie restriction can massively affect daily activities and reduce productivity. If your job involves a lot of physical and arduous work, this is not for you. Individuals with active jobs like department store employees, delivery workers, or others who perform vigorous physical activities need to consume more calories. Since the Sirtfood Diet drastically restricts your calorie intake (only 1000 calories per day in the first week), this is too little for highly active lifestyles. Failing to grant the necessary number of calories to your body than it requires for demanding activities, can lead to harsh health repercussions.

This also goes to individuals who perform high-intensity exercises every day, especially those requiring over 300 to 500 calories per session (depending on age, weight, and height of the individual). Even though staying active is necessary, it is crucial to ensure that your body is not experiencing additional stress while following this diet.

2. Do You Suffer From Medical Issues?

Individuals suffering from any medical complications are advised against following this eating plan. For instance, individuals with kidney issues can be majorly affected by this diet. Since dehydration and mass muscle loss are common side effects of following this, you need to be sure before you step ahead. People with diabetes shouldn't follow this diet either. Because sirtfood nutritional plans require consuming a fixed measure of carbohydrates, any amount above or below this designated threshold can worsen the condition of people with diabetes.

3. Consider Your Physical Attributes

Since this plan mainly focuses on calorie restriction and including sirtfoods, it can bring about different results for particular people. For instance, individuals who are overweight or who are very muscular need more calories during the day. People with a wider frame also need more calories to sustain their bodies throughout the day.

Gender also plays a role on calorie intake. Since women need fewer calories than men to sustain themselves throughout the day, they can more easily endure this diet compared to men. Further, because the Sirtfood Diet comprises a fixed calorie intake for everyone, people with a wider or taller frame may not be able to follow it. For instance, women who are 5-feet tall can comfortably go through the day with only 1000 calories; however, men who are 6-feet tall need over 1000 calories, even on weight loss programs. Basically, every individual needs a specific number of calories to, at least, cover their necessary daily activities. Anything less than that number can be dangerous for your health.

You can find online calculators to check the number of calories you need in a day based on your age, height, weight, and gender. Next, you need to calculate the number of calories you required for you to lose weight. If the number is higher than 1000 calories, avoid the diet.

So, before you begin, consider your physical attributes, age, and gender. If your attributes and number of calories needed partly align with the guidelines, you are good to go.

4. Do You Have Unhealthy Habits?

Unhealthy habits like smoking and drinking can hinder the results. These unhealthy habits can hinder *any* diet. When following a calorie-restricted nutrition plan that includes healthy ingredients (mainly vegetables, fruits, and lean protein), smoking and drinking can affect the positive effects you will see. While you are allowed a glass or two of red wine, increasing your alcohol intake or drinking alcoholic beverages with a high calorie count can cause weight gain as these drinks are mainly composed of empty calories. In addition, smoking can disturb your breathing pattern and disrupt the functioning of your lungs, which can cause an imbalance in other bodily functions, plus the massive amount of toxins it can accumulate in your body. These bad habits collectively cause weight gain and exacerbate various health issues, especially in the long run.

If you are guilty of these unhealthy habits, try quitting before you follow this diet. Even though it is difficult to quit them cold turkey, try taking one step at a time. Do this not only for the diet but also for your future health. This plan is a great way to eliminate unhealthy habits and to follow healthier eating patterns and a heartier lifestyle.

Since the Sirtfood Diet is a new trend in the fitness world, take all the necessary precautions before you delve deep into the experience to make sure this is a sustainable way of life for you. Since this diet mainly comprises around fruits, vegetables, cereals, and other healthy ingredients, it's not as restrictive as people think; it simply limits your intake to non-GMO foods and otherwise allows you to consume what you want in moderation. This diet plan has great anti-inflammatory, antioxidant, and anti-aging properties that sustain your health in the long run. You can always tweak the number of calories, ingredients, and other guidelines by a margin to follow the diet safely. Even if you cannot incorporate a lot of sirtfoods in your diet, sticking to the calorie restriction plan and eating as many healthy items as you can should do the trick.

SECTION TWO: Following the Diet

Now that you know the basics of the Sirtfood Diet, it's time to learn the practical aspects - incorporation, top sirtfoods, how to follow and sustain phases 1 and 2, a 21-day diet plan, and some recipes.

Chapter 5: Top 20 Sirtfoods

Before you create your shopping list, learn about the top 20 sirtfoods that are allowed to consume on this diet.

Let's take a look.

1. Kale

Any leafy greens is a boon for weight loss. Kale is pretty much incorporated into most diets, and on sirtfood-based nutritional plans, it's made into a juice consumed every day. Although it's unnecessary, it's highly recommended for weight loss, and it has numerous health benefits as it is packed with antioxidant properties. Kale is rich in two important components needed to lose weight: quercetin and kaempferol. These activate sirtuins in the body, which ultimately boosts metabolism.

This versatile ingredient can be used in various forms. One way is to chop it up, add lemon juice and olive oil, and serve it as a salad with other sirtfood ingredients. With two to four grams of dietary fiber in only one cup of kale, this fiber-dense ingredient keeps you full for some time. The high glucosinolate properties in kale provides anti-cancer and antioxidant properties. Last, the low-calorie content in kale keeps the daily and weekly calorie count in check.

2. Red Onions

Onions are one of the most crucial ingredients in cooking; it adds lots of flavor and is incredibly healthy. Unlike their white counterparts, red onions are not as spicy and have a sweet aftertaste to them. They can be used in cooking or eaten raw. Red onions are high in soluble fiber, which improves bowel movement and keeps you full. Further, fiber is an essential component of weight loss. A red onion contains around 3 grams of fiber.

And red onions are low in calories and are great for a calorie-restricted diet. One cup of chopped onions contains only around 64 calories. Try eating them raw with your meals or add them to your healthy sandwiches.

3. Strawberries

Who doesn't like strawberries? Why not serve this savory fruit with different desserts. It is one of the most popular sirtfoods on the list because it can be eaten and juiced. Strawberries are rich in antioxidants and they flush out harmful waste from the body. This you not only helps lose weight but also improves your skin and hair texture. Detoxification rejuvenates your cells and halts the aging process.

Compared to other fruits, strawberries contain a low sugar amount – around 1 tsp of fructose per 100 grams, which is almost negligible. This is nothing like artificial sugar, which should be eliminated from your diet completely. Artificial sugar, which is known as sucrose, could cause your skin and body to age while adding empty calories to your diet. But fruits such as strawberries are a healthy source of natural sugar and will help you feel rejuvenated and energetic on a low-calorie diet.

You can add it to your smoothies, your salads, or include them in healthy pancakes with made with buckwheat (another sirtfood); the options are limitless. By consuming strawberries, you are training your body to absorb sugary carbs and to handle them well.

4. Wine

Contrary to popular belief, wine, if consumed in moderation, is healthy for your body. It is one of the sirtfoods that attracts most dieters and fitness enthusiasts to try the diet. Red wine offers a myriad of health benefits, such as improving skin texture, cell regeneration, and even weight loss. Red wine consists of an important polyphenol called resveratrol, which offers anti-aging properties.

This component fights skin diseases and keeps wrinkles and fine lines at bay. Pinot noir should be your top choice of red wine on the Sirtfood Diet, as it contains a generous amount of resveratrol. Drink one to two glasses of red wine every day, or every other day, to lose weight.

5. Matcha Green Tea (or Simple Green Tea)

While matcha green tea is a lesser-known ingredient, it is a popular addition to health and fitness, and rightly so. Matcha is a concentrate of green tea, which is packed with nutrients and all the benefits of the standard green tea beverage. Young green tea leaves are treated and ground and then extracted in the form of a bright green powder. This can be consumed by adding and mixing it to hot water, just like green tea.

Matcha is rich in antioxidant properties (much more so than green tea due to its concentrated form) and it promotes weight loss. This green powder is also known to improve your metabolism and exercise endurance, which helps you burn more calories. You should be able to find matcha green tea in your local Asian store or order it online. This ingredient is actively used in the sirtfood green juice. Mix ½ tsp of this matcha green tea in hot water and consume it two times a day.

6. Dark Chocolate (85% Cocoa)

Another favorite item on the list, dark chocolate, is a top choice for dieters who find it difficult to fight cravings. Chocolate with at least 85% cocoa regulates heart health and stabilizes blood pressure. The bittersweet ingredient is loaded with antioxidants that flush out toxins from the body and prepare it for weight loss. And it reduces and fight off diseases, reduce oxidation, and boost immune systems. Dark chocolate contains a compound called flavanols, which regulates blood flow.

Track your intake as it is rich in calorie count. Do not consume over 1 or 2 pieces of dark chocolate a day, as it will cover most of your total calorie count. Since the Sirtfood Diet strictly focuses on calorie restriction, take extra care while consuming dark chocolate as one piece will account for 55 to 60 calories.

7. Extra Virgin Olive Oil

Olive oil is rich in healthy fats (monounsaturated fatty acids or MUFA) needed to keep your blood sugar levels balanced and maintain your heart health. Since it has a heavier base, it keeps you full for some time and reduces cravings. Extra virgin olive oil is made by pressing olives and using the extracted fat, which is healthy for your body. This olive oil choice is healthier as it is unprocessed and unrefined.

Use extra virgin olive oil for cooking your meals or drizzle some on top of your salads. You could use this as a base for salad dressings. Besides being rich in healthy fat, extra virgin olive oil is rich in medium-chain triglycerides (MCTs) that promote the production of peptide YY. This hormone regulates your appetite and curbs your hunger. Since olive oil is also loaded with calories, it is advised to use this ingredient in moderation.

8. Parsley

Parsley is a garnishing herb in most dishes, but in this diet, we are also using it as an ingredient in the popular sirtfood green juice (the recipe will be given in the last chapter). Try other popular dishes such as sirtfood pesto by adding it with walnuts. With only 22 calories and 0.47 grams of fat in 1 cup of parsley, this ingredient is a perfect addition to any weight-loss diet. More important, it is rich in apigenin, which is a dietary flavonoid used to treat inflammation. It acts as an antioxidant that fights free radicals.

Further, the high fiber content in parsley regulates your bowel movements and improves digestion. Parsley is rich in iron content, which improves the process of cell regeneration and increases the production of red blood cells. Luckily, incorporating parsley in your diet is easy due to its versatility.

9. Soy

Soy is rich in protein; it repairs and builds muscles and tissues, which helps burn fat and lose more weight. Protein is one of the essential components required weight loss. Since soy comprises high-quality protein, it supports the main bodily functions responsible for your metabolic rate and improvement in body composition. For vegetarians, this is a great replacement for meat and fish.

The best way to use soy is to ferment it and turn it into miso. Miso is a delicious Japanese fermented condiment that can be used in soups, salads, and stir-fries. Since soy and miso are loaded with sirtuin activators, these should be added in your Sirtfood Diet.

10. Blueberries

Berries are a crucial part of every weight-loss diet, mainly for two reasons – they are low in calories and high in antioxidant properties. Berries help detoxify the body and flush out harmful toxins in perspiration, urination, or any other form of excretion. This ingredient is an excellent addition to your breakfast as it tastes fantastic and enhances your smoothies or any other savory-sweet recipes. Blueberries are also rich in Vitamin C and K, dietary fiber, copper, and manganese. This tiny fruit protects the cellular structure and avoids damage by neutralizing free radicals.

Blueberries are low in calories, which makes it an ideal option for weight loss. Whether eaten raw or added to recipes, blueberries assist in burning stomach fat. Since blueberries are rich in calcium content, they can prevent osteoporosis and they strengthen bone density. Blueberries are packed with properties that target the skinny gene and accelerate fat-burning. They are useful if you suffer from increased abdominal and belly fat.

11. Red Chicory

Red chicory, also known as chicory root, has been in use for centuries for its medicinal properties and several health benefits. Since it is low in calories, it is an ideal addition to this calorie-restricted diet. Red chicory curbs appetite and reduce your food intake, which reduces your calorie intake. It is believed this ingredient reduces the secretion of the hunger hormone, ghrelin.

Further, red chicory improves blood sugar levels and boost digestive health. If you suffer from digestive issues, constipation, or diarrhea, this ingredient should be your go-to. Last, chicory root is rich in inulin, a fiber in your body with probiotic properties. It fights harmful bacteria and gives room for good microbes to develop and colonize. Red chicory improves digestive health, regulates blood sugar levels, improves mineral absorption, and reduces inflammation, which are all necessary for weight loss. If you cannot find red chicory in your area, yellow chicory is a good alternative.

12. Coffee

This is a controversial addition to the list of top sirtfoods that help lose weight. Coffee contains caffeine, which increases energy levels and improves physical performance. Since you will include exercise in your Sirtfood Diet, the caffeine content will help improve your performance and burn more calories. It has been proven that coffee drinkers are usually at a lesser risk of developing Type 2 diabetes.

Your brown fat, or brown adipose tissue, burns at an accelerated pace after drinking coffee; this burns more calories. Body heat is produced by burning fat and sugar, which eventually causes weight loss. Since brown fat causes weight gain, melting more brown fat should be your goal. Apart from this, coffee also contains antioxidant properties that fight free radicals.

13. Walnuts

It is believed that eating too many walnuts, or any other nut, might cause weight gain. While it is true that consuming extra calories can add pounds, walnuts can help you lose weight. It is one of the most popular sirtfoods that can be eaten as a snack or added to your breakfast smoothie. When paired with chocolate, it enhances the flavor of any dessert. While walnuts contain high-fat content and calories, they may still aid in weight loss.

This is because walnuts are high in protein content that helps repair muscles and tissues, and fiber, which keeps you feeling full for longer. And this ingredient is rich in antioxidants, helping your body to flush out harmful toxins and prepare it for weight loss. One antioxidant type present in walnuts, the polyphenol antioxidant, retains the elasticity of blood cells and protects them from damage.

14. Turmeric

Besides fruits and vegetables rich in polyphenols, we also have this golden ingredient that is also a staple in Asian and Middle Eastern cooking, and for the right reasons. Turmeric contains anti-inflammatory properties known to reduce bloating and inflammation; it helps maintain your body weight and lowers the chances of obesity. Further, it boosts immune health and reduces the risk of cancer. This is all thanks to a substance called curcumin, which has anti-inflammatory and anti-cancer properties.

Turmeric can be added to almost every savory recipe. Although, since curcumin is a bit difficult to digest, it might trigger digestive issues in some individuals. To make absorption easy, use turmeric with some fatty ingredients in your cooking. You can add a dash of black pepper to increase its digestion in your body. Among the myriad of spices available, turmeric is an effective sirtfood that should be added to your list.

15. Buckwheat

Buckwheat has been a popular ingredient in the world of health and fitness. It is rich in protein content and helps repair and build tissues and muscles. Well-built muscles are required in the process burning fat and achieving a lean and toned look. And buckwheat improves digestive health and regulates bowel movements. It offers a suitable environment for the microflora to grow, which aids in improving digestion. Besides promoting a healthy system, it also reduces cravings and curbs your appetite. If you feel hungry or crave food, feed on some buckwheat to sustain you for a longer.

Here's the best part about buckwheat – it can be added to almost every savory dish. Add it to your salad or mix it with your porridge; this can be a delicious and healthy ingredient that assists in weight loss. You can also prepare desserts using this versatile ingredient. It's always useful to have a little in your pantry if you are trying to lose weight.

16. Arugula (Rocket)

This peppery, leafy green vegetable is a delicious addition to your sirtfood meal plan. This versatile ingredient can be added to your salad, soup, or any other savory meal. Since arugula is 90% water content, it fills you up fast and reduces cravings; this helps curb your appetite, and you eat less. Ultimately, you will consume fewer calories, which will help you lose weight. The indole-3-carbinol and isothiocyanate compounds present in arugula induce anti-inflammatory properties also beneficial in weight loss.

Arugula is rich in phytochemical's, which generate antioxidant properties and neutralize radical damage. All these collectively prepare the body for weight loss. Additionally, arugula is rich in nutrients such as Vitamin K, Vitamin B, and folate. Vitamin K increases the absorption of calcium in your body, which reduces the risk of bone deterioration. Last, arugula is extremely low in calories. One cup of this bright, leafy vegetable contains only 40 calories, making it a suitable option for a calorie-restricted diet.

17. Capers

Capers are tiny, green flower buds extracted from the capers bush (also known as Flinders Rose). These are native to some parts of Europe, Asia, and Australia. Capers are sweet and salty in taste, making them a great addition to savory dishes, such as pasta and salads. When picked right off the caper bush, these caper buds can be too bitter, so they are mostly pickled. During the pickling process, these buds mellow down in taste and acquire a salty flavor.

Capers are rich in antioxidants and anti-inflammatory properties, which, as you know, are useful in losing weight and boosting metabolic health. Just 100 grams of capers have about 23 calories, which is a great addition to calorie-restricted diets like the Sirtfood Diet. Other important ingredients in capers are rutin and quercetin, which contain antibacterial properties and help fight cancer. Additionally, these components regulate blood circulation and lower bad cholesterol levels.

18. Bird's-Eye Chili

Any spicy component, when added to meals, helps in boosting metabolism and burning more calories. Bird's-eye chili is a type of chili smaller in size (2 to 3 cm in length) and is commonly found in Southeast Asian countries like India. These chilies have a pungent smell and a sharp taste, making them an apt ingredient for traditional dishes. This ingredient is also composed of capsaicin, an active component in most chilies that helps you lose weight. When activated, it increases body heat, which speeds up your metabolism. A higher metabolic rate burns more calories that eventually helps you lose more weight. In fact, the higher the metabolic rate, the more calories you can burn, and the more weight you can lose.

Even if it is too spicy for you, you can add chilies in your meals in moderation, and once you get used to the heat, incorporate it into your diet plan regularly. If you prefer, you can also eat them raw. Just 1 or 2 chilies are enough to increase body heat. Plus, they are extremely low in calories.

19. Medjool Dates

Medjool dates are a super-tasty addition to your list of sirtfoods. These are soft, sweet, gooey, and taste just like regular dates. Some individuals prefer not to eat dates as they are believed to be high in sugar, but if eaten in moderation, these will help you lose weight. Medjool dates are rich in essential minerals, such as Vitamin B6, magnesium, copper, and potassium. This ingredient keeps blood sugar levels in check (despite being high in sugar content) and promotes a healthy nervous system.

You can eat these as a snack or chop them up and add them to your salad. Since they are high in fiber, eating 1 or 2 of these post-lunch will fight cravings and curb your appetite until your next meal. Additionally, the fiber content prevents sudden spikes in insulin levels and balances the blood sugar.

20. Lovage

Lovage is a less-known herb that is, in fact, one of the most useful food items for weight loss. It is rich in antioxidants, one of which is quercetin. This component reduces inflammation in your body, boosts physical performance, and fights free radicals. All these benefits are useful to those losing weight. It is easy to confuse lovage with parsley and celery as they look and feel the same, but lovage has a mild taste of aniseed, which makes it easy to distinguish.

This herb is versatile and can be used in several ways, such as in a salad, adding it to your omelet, or combining it with roast chicken. Lovage has a pleasant aroma that can enhance the taste of almost any dish.

These top 20 sirtfoods should be included in your meal plan. As you can see, these foods help in losing weight and improve your overall health. These items are collectively useful for weight loss, balancing blood sugar levels, improving digestion, boosting immunity, and elevating your bodily performance. Regular consumption of these food items will cause better physical and mental health.

Chapter 6: Phase 1: Getting Started

The Sirtfood Diet is divided into two phases based on the number of calories and types of meals to be consumed throughout the day. In this chapter, let's consider Phase 1, which covers the first 3 days of your Sirtfood Diet. If followed religiously, this stage can help you lose over seven pounds in seven days. Pay attention to this phase and try to follow the guidelines diligently.

Phase 1 Plan

During the first 3 days, you are allowed three sirtfood green juices along with one full sirtfood meal. These juices and meals are distributed over 1000 calories throughout the day. It is recommended to have the full meal for lunch as dinners should often be light when you're dieting. It depends on your preference, you can eat the whole meal for dinner instead of lunch if you prefer.

Day 3 to 7 are more lenient, and you may eat 1500 calories daily that must be distributed among two meals and two green juices throughout the eating period. This phase is bound to work because no matter what you consume, a 1000-calorie plan will show effective results (in terms of losing weight).

The following is how you will generally experience your first three days, or Phase 1 of the Sirtfood Diet.

Day 1 - 1,000 Calories (three Juices, one Meal)

You begin your morning with a green juice for breakfast. The juice, which normally comprises kale, parsley, arugula, celery, ginger, lemon, matcha green tea, and a small piece of green apple, is an effective way to lose weight. It also promotes digestion, improves your skin texture, boosts immunity, and curbs appetite. The high fiber content in this juice keeps you full for longer and help you get to the next meal with no hassles. One glass of this green juice consists of approximately one hundred calories, which is relatively low compared to the satiating feeling it provides.

To increase the gap between your meals, try to have the drink late in the morning, say around 10 am. As soon as you wake up, drink tea or warm water with added lemon; this boosts the fat burning process and satiate your hunger until breakfast time. If needed, have an espresso before your first meal, or add a tiny amount of protein with your green juice. For instance, you can have a hard-boiled egg with your juice for breakfast; this keeps hunger pangs at bay and keeps you going, but make sure that your meal's added ingredient doesn't push your calorie count past the 1,000 for the day.

This juice in the morning should sustain you until lunch. Have the second green juice for lunch at 2 or 3 pm. Your snack will include one square of dark chocolate with at least 85% cocoa. If your calorie count allows, add a small bowl of shelled edamame as a snack. Have your third green juice as an evening snack. Your dinner meal can be anything sirtfood-friendly (either stick to the plan provided later or choose from the recipes you will learn in the last chapter). Again, the most important thing to remember is to be within the 1,000-calorie count.

Further, don't forget to consume loads of water. Drink at least 8 to 10 glasses or more throughout the day. The more water you have, the easier it should be for you to lose weight. At times, you will feel hunger pangs or crave something decadent. Drinking a glass of water during these moments will keep you satiated and keep the cravings away. Sometimes, your body confuses thirst for hunger. What you actually need is water; drink a glass, and if you still feel hungry, grab a fruit or a low-calorie snack. Again, make sure that it fits within your calorie count.

On Day 1, you might also note frequent cravings, partly because of hunger and majorly because of old habits. On typical days, we are bound to grab a bite when we feel bored, which is advised against on this plan. Due to familiar routines, you might look for snacks out of boredom. If you cannot resist, don't fight it, eat a light snack, or divide your juices in two.

So, your day 1 looks like this: three green juices, one espresso, one hard-boiled egg, one sirtfood meal, and snacks like one square of dark chocolate or one bowl of shelled edamame.

Day 2 – 1,000 Calories (three Juices, one Meal)

Day two looks similar to Day one, but today you should feel lighter and motivated to continue your plan. Follow the same schedule as Day one with the lemon water, espresso, or green tea to begin your morning. Have a glass of green juice for breakfast, followed by a mid-morning snack like a boiled egg or a small portion of chicken. Next, have another glass of juice for lunch and one piece of dark chocolate for your evening snack. If need be, have a cup of espresso.

If you are hungry at any point during the day, grab a medium-sized fruit low in calories. But if you are not hungry and cannot finish your green juice, do not force yourself. Have as much as you can and leave it for the next day.

Again, don't forget to drink loads of water. Since this green juice is rich in fiber and is heavy, you might feel full with only half a glass. If that's the case, divide it into smaller portions and consume it throughout the day. By doing this, you not only keep cravings away, but also feel energetic throughout the day.

On Day 2, prepare another delicious and nutritious sirtfood meal for lunch or dinner (choose any recipe from the last chapter). Again, make sure that your meals are complying with the 1,000-calorie mark per day. Your main sirtfood meal can either be vegan or vegetarian or a piece of lean meat or fish. For more variety, mix and match your options to cut the monotony and stick to your diet.

Similar to Day 1, your day two will look like this: three green juices, one espresso, one hard-boiled egg, one sirtfood meal, and snacks like one square of dark chocolate or one bowl of shelled edamame. You can also incorporate a medium-sized fruit if you feel too hungry.

Day 3 – 1,000 Calories (3 Juices, 1 Meal)

The third day of your Sirtfood Diet will feel light and notice a massive loss in weight. It is recommended to check up on your weight once the first week passes.

Start your morning with warm lemon water, espresso, or green tea. Have a glass of green juice for breakfast, followed by a mid-morning snack like a boiled egg or a small portion of chicken. Prepare a sirtfood meal for lunch or dinner and incorporate a piece of dark chocolate with a fruit or a cup of espresso. Add a modest bowl of shelled edamame if you feel too hungry. You are also allowed another square of dark chocolate for dessert.

If you can drink the green juices feeling no gagging sensation, it means that your body is accepting it. If not, you will feel like throwing up immediately after taking a few sips of this juice. To avoid this sensitivity and prepare your body to accept the green juice, make a fresh batch every time. You can also change the measurements of the ingredients. For instance, if you don't like the flavor of kale and if it makes you gag, increase the amount of green apple. Instead of adding a quarter of an apple, add half. Similarly, tweak the other ingredients. Also make sure that you adhere to the calorie count, nutritional quality, and quantity of the juice.

By the end of the third day, your stomach should be acquainted with the new style of eating and healthy meals. For this reason, you feel fewer hunger pangs and more energetic throughout the afternoon. Some individuals are so full throughout the day and find they cannot finish the third glass of green juice. Drink 8 to 10 glasses of water daily. Since alcohol is not allowed during the first week of this diet, you must wait a week to enjoy your occasional glass of red wine. Remember, you can have any amount of water, coffee, and green tea (as these are lower in calorie count).

Your typical timings over the first few days can look like this:

7:30 a.m.: 1 glass of warm water with freshly squeezed lemon juice

10 a.m.: First glass of green juice

2:30 p.m.: Second glass of green juice

4 p.m.: Snack (dark chocolate with espresso or shelled edamame)

6 p.m.: Third glass of green juice

9 p.m.: Sirtfood meal

You can also substitute the 4 p.m. snack with a third glass of green juice and push the sirtfood meal ahead to 7:30 pm. You can have the dark chocolate as a post-dinner dessert. Adjust the timings according to your sleeping and waking schedules and according to your old eating habits. Spread the juices, snacks, and meals across the day as you prefer, if you feel like this could keep your hunger pangs under control.

Your third day looks like this – 3 green juices, one espresso, one hard-boiled egg, one sirtfood meal, and snacks such as one square of dark chocolate or one bowl of shelled edamame, and another dark chocolate square for dessert.

Day 4 - 1,500 Calories (2 Juices, 2 Meals)

With the first 3 days gone, you have successfully endured the most difficult part of the plan. Day 4 allows you to eat 1500 calories, distributed among two meals, two juices, and some snacks. Consume one glass of juice for breakfast and one as a snack. Try to eliminate snacks today as they could go over the calorie limit, but if your sirtfood meals give some room to accommodate extra snacks, such as a piece of dark chocolate or a bowl of shelled edamame, go for it. Since all your meals are nutrient-rich and high in fiber content, these should sustain you.

Instead of having a third glass of juice, try to incorporate this recipe into your meal and turn it into a salad. Ingredients such as kale, celery, rocket, parsley, and apple are an integral part of a healthy salad. You can also add walnuts and a dressing made from fresh lemon juice and extra virgin olive oil. This meal can be substituted for one of your sirtfood meals. It is recommended to have it for dinner since lighter.

Spread a bed of kale on a plate and drizzle a little olive oil and lemon dressing over it. Using your hands, spread the oil over the kale until the leaves absorb the flavor from the dressing.

If you feel hungry between eating, drink more water. Consume enough water throughout the day, at least 2 to 3 liters.

Your fourth day looks like this - 2 green juices, one espresso, two sirtfood meals, and snacks such as one square of dark chocolate or one bowl of shelled edamame.

Day 5 - 1,500 Calories (2 Juices, 2 Meals)

To keep your stomach full and avoid cravings, assign one of your daily meals to breakfast and have the other meal for lunch or dinner. Your breakfast can be sirtfood muesli or sirtfood blueberry pancakes. For the second meal, experiment with other sirtfood ingredients or pepper your existing meals with sirtfoods. Certain ingredients that also activate sirtuins can be easily incorporated or replaced in your meals. For instance, have buckwheat instead of rice; the goal is to cram in as many sirtfoods as possible, but keep your options open and try new recipes every day. The same ingredients can get too boring, and you could even end the diet at this pace. For this reason, maintain variation in your diet and ensure that you add as many sirtfoods as possible.

Further, make sure to sip water every once in a while. Keep a bottle of water handy by your side and take sips of liquid even if you are not thirsty. Don't forget the best part of your daily diet: the two squares of dark chocolate post-dinner or as snacks.

Your fifth day looks like this – 2 green juices, one espresso, one hard-boiled egg, two sirtfood meals, and snacks such as one square of dark chocolate or one bowl of shelled edamame.

Day 6 – 1,500 Calories (2 Juices, 2 Meals)

You follow the same routine on Day 6. If you work in an office or need to eat lunch outside, pack your lunch to avoid having to order food that doesn't comply with these dietary restrictions. Have your green juices at home to have them fresh.

Apart from incorporating sirtfoods in your eating habits, it is also essential to balance your meals with adequate macronutrients. To do this, look at the sirtfoods you may consume and divide them according to carbs, protein, and healthy fat. Try to include a generous amount of protein in your diet as it will keep you satiated and help build muscle. The more muscle you build, the more fat you burn, which causes a steady fall in your body weight. Some protein-rich sirtfoods you can have on your diet include chicken, lentils, tuna, or smoked salmon.

If you are unsure what to cook, simply grill some chicken and add it to a bed of sirtfood green leaves, such as rocket leaves or kale, accompanied by a dressing of olive oil and lemon juice. This is an easy way to incorporate a healthy meal into your diet and still abide by the Sirtfood Diet guidelines. To make the process simpler, grill some chicken beforehand and store it. When time for your meal, warm it up and add it to your salad for lunch or dinner.

Again, don't forget to drink 8 to 10 glasses of water to keep your metabolic rate in check and avoid water retention.

Further, start your day with a glass of warm water and fresh lemon juice. Since your breakfast will be relatively heavy during the next 4 days of your diet, you can easily find yourself satiated until time for lunch. Have a cup of espresso or green tea along with a low-calorie snack as a mid-morning or evening snack. As mentioned, make sure to reach the recommended calorie count without going over it by a long shot.

Your sixth day looks like this - 2 green juices, one espresso, one hard-boiled egg, two sirtfood meals, and snacks such as one square of dark chocolate or one bowl of shelled edamame.

Day 7 - 1,500 Calories (2 Juices, 2 Meals)

If your seventh day of the diet falls on a weekend, you, unfortunately, cannot have a cheat meal or exceed your calories even for one day. Since this plan requires you to follow a strict regime for 21 days, there are no cheat meals allowed within this period, however you can substitute ingredients of your favorite recipes with sirtfoods. For instance, use rocket leaves as a topping for pizza and add turmeric or bird's-eye chili in your savory meals. That's the best part about the Sirtfood Diet - the ingredients included in this diet are so versatile that you can use them to create any delicious dish.

If you feel the urge to snack, have 1 or 2 sirtfood bites (made of cocoa and walnuts - find the recipe below) or have a home-made granola bar. This treat may not seem like enough, but it effectively fights cravings and curbs appetite. And to indulge in your "treat" you can also add a slice or two of toast that don't exceed your daily calorie count significantly. Even if you do go over the calorie mark by a margin, incorporate light exercise, such as walking, jogging, or yoga to burn those extra calories and keep yourself on track.

Your snacks can include a handful of walnuts, capers, or two pieces of 85% cocoa dark chocolate.

Your seventh day looks like this – 2 green juices, one espresso, two sirtfood meals, and snacks such as two squares of dark chocolate or a handful of walnuts or capers.

Once your 7 days are over, check your weight on the scale. You will notice a drop that ranges from 5 to 10 pounds, depending on your age, weight, height, and body type. Even if you don't notice a major loss, do not panic as you might have just put on some muscle mass, which is necessary to achieve a toned look and to burn more fat. As long as you are following the plan religiously, you will inevitably lose weight.

You can either take up some mild exercises like walking or yoga or skip the routine entirely. Since you are on a strict calorie restriction (at least for the first 3 days of your diet), you will automatically lose weight.

Insights or Experiences after Phase 1

Once you successfully complete the first week of the Sirtfood Diet, your entire outlook regarding diet, fitness, and healthy eating will change. Not only because of the amount of weight you will lose but also because of the notable changes you will see and feel in your body.

However, let's talk about some real-life experiences or obstacles that could arise after Phase 1 passes.

Monotony or Repetition of Ingredients

Even though you may have twenty types of sirtfoods in your diet, only ten of these are readily available or can be freely added to your meals. Some of these ingredients include kale, buckwheat, rocket leaves, celery, and turmeric. Adding these to your daily meals can be too boring and monotonous, at least starting the 4th or 5th day. Surviving on these ingredients for the rest of the 21 days in your diet might seem difficult. The best way to overcome this monotony is by switching between vegan and meat meals now and then. It might sound severe, but you can include variety in your diet by planning and prepping the ingredients beforehand. Mixing and matching is key to consistently following this diet.

Unbalanced Portion Sizes

On the Sirtfood Diet, you either have too much food to consume or too little to satisfy your hunger. This can majorly affect your eating patterns and throw you off guard on particular days. For instance, the first three days of week 1 requires you to have only 1,000 calories a day, which is often not enough to keep you feeling full; and with the green juices that can be gulped down within a few minutes, you'll find that your stomach growls sometimes. But you suddenly jump to an additional 500 calories from Day 4, and you have to feed on two heavy sirtfood meals that can be too harsh for your newly developed eating pattern.

On some days, you might also feel that portion sizes are too large, which makes you rethink your diet decisions. Since you feel heavy and satiated, you might question the effectiveness of this diet. If so, divide your meals into smaller portions and spread them throughout the day. This will keep your stomach full, but you will feel light. Further, use ingredients in the correct quantity. Adding too much kale just because it is low in calories isn't wise; the high amount of fiber in green leafy vegetables makes it filling, so a small amount can go a long way without shocking your body with an overabundance of fiber that can cause digestive issues. Stick to the suggested amounts of each ingredient and do not exceed them. If you add too much of the same ingredient, this will increase your calorie count for the day, defeating this diet's purpose. On the flipside, if you feel you are not full enough, spreading meals across the day can be very effective in keeping you satiated for longer.

Enjoy Shopping and Meal Planning

Since you will have enough time to shop for ingredients and plan your meals, you can easily make informed decisions and enjoy the process. The Sirtfood Diet is a 21-day diet process. You can begin whenever you have the time.

You will be buying your ingredients beforehand according to your nutrition plan, so your chances of sticking to the diet will increase drastically. Consider the upcoming week and plan your means and buy ingredients for the next week ahead. Prepping your ingredients saves time for you to do cooking and preparing your meals.

If you show enough dedication, patience, and willpower during the first week, you will most likely go through these weeks with little hassle. Pay attention to your eating habits, count your calories, and drink a few glasses of green juice every day. Even though it is easier said than done, all you need to think about are the end results to keep going.

Chapter 7: Phase 2: Maintenance

Getting started is the easy part; the real challenge is in maintaining it. Since the Sirtfood Diet eliminates major food groups and reduces your calorie intake by a large margin, it can be a bit difficult to maintain for longer periods. However, individuals concerned about frequent cravings on the diet have nothing to worry about as they are allowed wine and chocolate, which helps fight cravings and supports the new weight.

The second step of the Sirtfood Diet is the maintenance phase, which occurs over the next 14 days. Your diet's success and the weight you lose over a prolonged period depend on this phase. The dieter can eat three sirtfood meals per day and still have one green juice per day.

Phase 2 of the Sirtfood Diet

Follow this plan to get started with Phase 2:

With the onset of Phase 2, you may eat three sirtfood meals and one green juice throughout the day. It begins on the eighth day of your Sirtfood Diet and ends on the 21st day.

This is how you typically experience your first 3 days.

Day 8 – 1,500 to 1,700 Calories (3 Meals, 1 Green Juice)

On Day 8, you can have a glass of red wine, 6 oz (if you are open to choices, Pinot noir is the best kind as it is high in sirtuins). By this time, your body will have been acquainted with the new eating pattern, which is why alcohol can be easily included in the diet.

Your eighth day looks like this – 1 green juice, 1 espresso, 1 hard-boiled egg, 3 sirtfood meals, and snacks such as 1 square of dark chocolate, walnut halves, a bowl of blueberries, or shelled edamame.

Day 9 – 1,500 to 1,700 Calories (3 Meals, 1 Green Juice)

By Day 9, your digestive system will have been acquainted with your new eating pattern, which will reduce cravings by a significant margin. Your occasional desire for sugar and snacks will majorly or entirely vanish, and you should feel more at ease with your new eating habits.

Your ninth day looks like this – 1 green juice, one cup espresso or green tea, three sirtfood meals, and snacks like one square of dark chocolate, walnut halves, or one bowl of shelled edamame.

Day 10 to Day 20 – 1,500 Calories to 1,700 Calories (3 Meals, 1 Green Juice)

The next 2 weeks will follow the same pattern. Although, you can juggle between the meals and snack options. Follow the 21-day diet plan below. You can also prepare a personalized meal plan depending on the ingredients you prefer along with the flexibility you have. Just make sure these fall between 1,500 to 1,700 calories. Don't forget to add one glass of green juice.

Your days 10 to 20 look like this – 1 green juice, 3 sirtfood meals, and snacks such as:

- 1 or 2 squares of dark chocolate
- 1 bowl of shelled edamame
- 2 to 3 hard-boiled eggs (mostly whites)

- Sirtfood bites
- Sirtfood granola bars
- A small bowl of blueberries or strawberries
- Any medium-sized fruit
- 2 to 4 walnut halves

Add any other healthy snack of your choice. The best way is to incorporate various sirtfoods is through snacks. There are many breakfast, lunch, and dinner recipes to choose from. Follow the 21-day Sirtfood Diet plan below or make your own plan with the recipes offered in the last chapter. If you feel hungry between meals, have a cup of espresso or green tea. You can also have a glass of red wine whenever you please (if it doesn't exceed the calorie count). Try to stick to 1 glass of red wine per day. You are allowed 2 to 3 glasses of red wine weekly, so adjust accordingly.

Day 21 – 1,500 to 1,700 Calories (3 Meals, 1 Green Juice)

The 21st day is your last day of this journey. Since you have been following the Sirtfood Diet for a while now, this day should go smoothly. Follow your everyday routine and have three sirtfood meals with one green juice.

By the end of your 21st day, you will feel lighter, energetic, and notice a major change in your body weight. Further, by the time you reach the last day, you have developed a healthy eating habit and pattern you want to follow for as long as possible.

Your day 21 looks like this – 1 green juice, 1 espresso, 3 sirtfood meals, and a snack such as dark chocolate squares or walnut halves.

This is just a rough plan for you to get started. Keep reading to for a detailed meal plan you can follow effortlessly.

Another important note: try to drink at least 8 to 10 cups of water throughout the day. Water keeps you satiated, curbs appetite, improves skin texture, and boosts weight loss. Another important thing to consider is the freshness of the green juice you're consuming. Since you'll be having this juice every day, you can prepare it in bulk and store it for consumption over the next few days. You can juice a fresh glass every time you have to drink it. Preparing a fresh glass of juice right before consumption is highly recommended as it retains the taste and nutrition of the ingredients. If you do not have enough time, juice 1 or 2 glasses in the morning, and consume them over the day. Try not to prepare them in bulk as the ingredients lose freshness and nutritional value.

Investing in a heavy-duty blender is highly recommended. Prepare your ingredients beforehand, such as peeling the ginger skin and having the ingredients ready. You have only to throw them in and blend them and your fresh juice will be prepared within 2 to 3 minutes.

Once you complete the first two phases successfully, you can focus more on *what* you are eating instead of *how much* you are consuming, which is also the ultimate goal of the Sirtfood Diet - healthy eating. By the end of the last day, you not only find you have lost a lot of weight, but you also see changes in your body. Your blood sugar levels will be in control, and you should notice an elevation in your energy levels. More important, you will feel healthy and look more radiant.

Since the Sirtfood Diet is based on calorie restriction, it is necessary to maintain this diet for a prolonged period because you can easily put on the weight back. Further, to see more benefits, follow this plan as a part of your lifestyle since short-term dieting doesn't show noticeable health changes except for weight loss.

The first 1 or 2 weeks are the most difficult to endure but the phases where you will notice how much weight you've lost. This is because your body loses its water weight at the beginning, which can return easily. If you increase your calorie intake or go back to your normal eating habits, all the water weight lost will return in a jiffy. To see long-term results and sustain the diet for a prolonged period, you need reliable ways to maintain it.

Here are a few tips that will help you maintain the Sirtfood Diet and lose more weight successfully.

Plan Your Meals

Meal planning is one of the easiest and most essential ways you can sustain your diet for a longer period. Once you know your weekly plan, it is easier to stick to it. Meal planning usually takes place in three stages – choosing your recipes, listing the ingredients required and buying them. You must also prepare these ingredients beforehand. By following these three steps, it is effortless to incorporate only healthy sirtfood meals in your diet. The main goal here is to keep you focused and to identify ways to stick to healthy eating habits.

In the upcoming chapters, you will learn how to plan your meals efficiently, the importance of doing so, a step-by-step approach to planning your meals, and a 21-day meal plan to kick-start your dieting journey. Some myths related to meal strategy will also be addressed in the coming chapters, which will motivate you to begin this process today and start your fitness journey with no ifs, ands, or buts.

Add Sirtfoods as a Regular Part of Your Meals

Now, the real question is – what should be done once the first two phases end?

Once this phase ends, there are no further instructions except how to continue eating a balanced diet that includes sirtfoods. Once activated, the inner sirtuin proteins start working, and you will merely need to continue incorporating sirtfoods to keep the engine running.

With this tip in mind, you can gain the benefits of sirtfoods and continue losing weight in the long run. By adding sirtfoods to your diet or replacing junk food with other healthy ingredients, you will notice a change in your body and weight while sustaining a healthy lifestyle. For instance, replace white rice and pasta with buckwheat, or add more turmeric powder or soy in your diet. Basically, switching to sirtfoods will enhance your eating habits and help you stay fitter. Add exercise in your daily routine and you will notice significant weight loss results. However, who wouldn't mind a glass of red wine a day? The best part about sirtfoods is these can be easily incorporated in your diet and all the options you have are delicious.

Add recipes made with sirtfoods. If you need ideas, go through the last chapter. Sirtfood recipes are enjoyable, healthy, versatile, and nutritious. Some of these recipes are probably much more interesting than your usual lunch and dinner meals. By incorporating these ideas, you are including more sirtfoods to your diet and adding variation to your daily meal plan. Since you are including these sirtfood meals in your weekly meals, you are automatically following the Sirtfood Diet. Start with a few sirtfood ingredients and include sirtfood recipes in your meals.

Exercise

Last, since there are no rules or instructions to follow after these 21 days, you can incorporate 30 to 45 minutes of exercise every day or 3 days a week to your routine. Exercising burns extra calories and helps you lose weight. For your exercise plan to work, it is necessary that you include sirtfood meals in your diet and stay away from junk foods. This will keep you energetic, increase metabolic rate, and help you burn more calories.

As you already know, regular exercise stimulates the activity of certain sirtuins, which protect the human body from premature aging. And they also preserve your body from degeneration and enhance your body's natural detoxification process.

In the upcoming chapters, you will find a detailed 21-day plan followed in accordance with these two phases, making sure to divide the number of calories and meals throughout each day.

Chapter 8: Incorporating Exercise

Incorporating exercise can double the results and boost your weight loss. While adding fitness is necessary even in your regular routine, it is specifically important on the Sirtfood Diet. Since Phase 1 of this diet keeps you on a strict calorie-restricted plan, you might not have enough energy to sustain physical activities during exercise. For this reason, it is advised to exercise with the onset of Phase 2 or 14 days after starting your diet.

Some individuals prefer to exercise from day 1 in Phase 1. To add exercise from the beginning, it is recommended to eat more calories from healthy food items. Although, to make the overall process safe and keep you from overeating or getting sick, it is advised to begin this routine only after 1 or 2 weeks of starting the diet.

Even in Phase 2, when you work out, stop if you feel fatigued or unwell. Do not put your body through additional stress as it could reverse the positive effects of the diet. For safe results, listen to your body and only exercise if you have the energy, but don't avoid movement simply because you're too lazy to exert extra effort. This way, you can burn additional calories and accelerate the weight loss journey.

Types of Exercises You Can Include on the Sirtfood Diet

If these exercises seem uninteresting or uncomfortable, you can also play a sport of your choosing. Or follow home workout videos you can find on YouTube. The important thing is to incorporate at least 30 to 45 minutes of movement into daily routine, despite the form. The ultimate goal is to burn more calories and speed up the weight loss process.

Here are some exercises that you can perform along with the duration and number of calories burned with each activity.

1. Walking or Jogging

Walking is the simplest form of exercise that can burn calories without putting your body under stress. It is a form of cardio that focuses on contouring your body through burning fat.

Aim at completing 7,000 to 8,000 steps every day to burn more calories. Although, since your body is deprived of calories in the initial stages, it is safe to stick with 5,000 steps. Once you jump to Phase 2 of your diet, you can incorporate jogging or running to increase the number of calories you burn. During Phase 2, aim at taking at least 10,000 steps daily. To avoid putting yourself under a lot of stress, try a combination of walking, trotting, and running. Once you incorporate walking in your daily routine, you can slowly build your way up to jogging and running to burn more calories.

Follow this weekly plan to start losing weight through this simple cardio exercise routine.

Monday: Warm-up for 5 minutes and take a brisk walk for 30 minutes.

Tuesday: Take the day off.

Wednesday: Warm-up for 5 minutes and take a brisk walk for 35 minutes.

Thursday: Warm-up for 5 minutes and take a brisk walk for 35 minutes. Jog for 1 minute and walk for 3 minutes.

Friday: Warm-up for 5 minutes and take a brisk walk for 45 minutes. Jog for 1 minute and walk for 2 minutes.

Saturday: Take the day off.

Sunday: Warm-up for 5 minutes and take a brisk walk for 60 minutes. Jog for 2 minutes and walk for 3 minutes.

Don't forget to stretch after every session.

Walking, jogging, and running are popular choices as they are no-cost exercises that burn a lot of calories compared to the amount of time put in, but if you suffer from knee-related or joint issues, avoid jogging and running as it could worsen your condition. All you need is a pair of comfortable tennis shoes to start. Get up early and go to your nearest park to practice your routines.

Duration: 60 minutes

Calories burned: 210 to 280 (at a speed of 3-mile per hour)

Suitable for: Phase 1 of the diet

2. HIIT

HIIT or High-Intensity Interval Training is the fastest way to burn serious calories. It demands short bursts of movements or exercises for a few seconds and a shorter or equal rest, after which the process continues. During these vigorous rounds of training, your heart rate rises, which increases your metabolic rate and burns calories faster. While it does expend a lot of energy and melts loads of calories, Sirtfood dieters should avoid performing HIIT in the first 2 weeks of their diet regime. HIIT exercises need you to put in a lot of power, and with the already reduced amount of calorie intake, you cannot cope.

As mentioned, HIIT should be performed only during Phase 2 of the Sirtfood Diet (even if you have been working on moderate exercises for a while). The reason fitness enthusiasts highly prefer HIIT is that it burns calories even after the session has ended.

Follow these basic HIIT exercises to start you with this exercise form.

Don't forget to warm up before you complete these exercises. Further, after every work out session, stretching is essential.

- **Mountain climbers:** Get on all fours and push your knees to your stomach while keeping your arms straight. Start in slow motion and increase your speed gradually as you go. As a start, perform three sets of 20 reps each. This exercise targets your core, arms, obliques, glutes, shoulders, and legs.

- **High knees:** Stand in an upright position and bring your knees as high as you can. Speed this up gradually and alternate knees. As a start, perform three sets of 15 reps with both legs.

- **Jumping jacks:** In this exercise, you jump while spreading your feet outwards then return to an upright position. As a start, perform three sets of 15 reps each.

- **Burpees:** Start with a plank position, then jump to touch the ceiling. Go back to the plank position and repeat. As a start, perform two sets of 10 reps each.

- **Lunges:** Lunges tone your quads, hamstrings, and hips. Use weights to burn more calories. As a start, perform three sets of 20 reps on each leg. With time, add heavier weights.

- **Push-ups:** Push-ups are the best exercise to tone up your core, arms, shoulders, and chest. As a start, perform three sets of 15 reps each.

Duration: 20 minutes

Calories burned: 150 to 180

Suitable for: Phase 2 of the diet

3. Pilates

Pilates is a lesser-known form of fitness as it is usually low impact and believed to burn fewer calories compared to other exercises. Since it is a low impact exercise, it can be easily incorporated into your exercise routine without stressing you out. It helps build lean muscles, tones your body, and improves your posture. Even though it will not burn more calories, it will help boost other bodily functions that support weight loss. However, if performed regularly, Pilates can help you lose weight.

As long as you achieve some mild form of exercise as opposed to none, you can consider Pilates as an effective weight loss boosting activity. If you still don't see results over time, you can combine Pilates with another form of cardio, aerobics, or weight training programs.

Pilates should be performed at least 2 to 3 times per week, or more often for better results. Once you are proficient with the basics, you can jump to the advanced version or combine exercise forms trending now, such as Yogalates (yoga and Pilates) and Piloxing (Pilates and boxing). With more practice, you will notice and experience elevated energy levels, improved posture, muscle development, and a stronger core.

Duration: 50 minutes

Calories burned: 175 (for a 150-pound person)

Suitable for: Phase 1 of the diet

4. Yoga

Yoga is yet another form of exercise that affects your physical and mental health. Even though yoga is slow to show visible toning, the effect is long-term. And yoga helps improve flexibility. For this exercise, you need to perform a set of postures or asanas targeted at specific body parts.

With regular practice, you will learn to practice mindfulness and acquire more patience. Yoga is an ideal choice for individuals on the Sirtfood Diet. It burns more calories without overworking your body and helps you become more patient in your journey. You will develop a stronger stamina and feel too motivated to give up easily. It is believed that regular yoga sessions keep you from binge eating and motivate you to eat healthy foods.

Another positive side effect of yoga is that it promotes sleep quality. It's no surprise that improved rest enhances weight loss results and burns more fat. Yoga also reduces stress, which is the number 1 enemy for your body's health. Increased stress levels result in poor eating habits, which ultimately result in weight gain. With yoga, you can calm your mind and diminish stress levels. If you are struggling with binge eating, yoga should be your go-to. Last, yoga improves your digestion and boosts your metabolism, which is also useful in weight loss programs.

Practice these poses or asanas every day to improve flexibility, elevate concentration levels, reduce stress, and burn fat.

• **Surya Namaskar or Sun Salutations:** This yoga form comprises 12 poses that move your entire body and target specific areas. Performing 108 rounds of Surya namaskars can burn a significant number of calories. It might need some practice and patience to perform 108 rounds every day. Start with three and add 2 to 5 rounds every day.

• **Chaturanga Dandasana or Plank pose:** This pose targets your abdominal muscles and improves flexibility around your belly. It's an effective posture to tone your core.

• **Trikonasana or Triangle pose:** In this pose, you twist your waist to be in a lateral position. Since it also involves stretching your thighs and hamstrings, it helps tone your lower body, too.

• **Sethu Bandha Sarvangasana or Bridge pose:** In this pose, you lie flat on the ground and lift your body up through your core and abdomen. This stretches your body, regulates hormones, and aids weight loss.

These are just some asanas for you to get started. If you like yoga and want to perform it for a prolonged period, incorporate other poses in your routine. To perform these asanas, all you need is a yoga mat, free space in your house, and possibly calming music.

Duration: 30 minutes

Calories burned: 100 to 120 (for a 125-pound person)

Suitable for: Phase 1 of the diet

5. Weight Training

Lifting weights is now a popular exercise form for most fitness enthusiasts. People used to believe that lifting weights would make a woman more muscular and bulkier, which is why only males resort to this exercise plan. Although lifting weights builds muscle, it won't make you look any more masculine. It develops more lean muscle, which burns more fat and gives the body a leaner, fitter, and toned look.

Just like HIIT, lifting weights demands a lot of calories. This is why you should start this exercise only in Phase 2 of your Sirtfood Diet. This has another added benefit, just like HIIT, which is increasing the resting metabolic rate and burning calories even when relaxing. It is believed that weightlifting can burn calories up to 38 hours after finishing a session. Weight training is one of the most effective weight loss exercises.

The best exercises in weight training help you move your body in every way. For instance, you move your legs, back, shoulders, arms, hips, hamstrings, and belly in the natural way they stretch, which builds muscles and tones your body when done regularly. Further, you'll get to perform different exercises such as lunging, squatting, bending, twisting, pulling, and pushing. These patterns, when followed with weights, tone your body and help you burn fat.

Incorporate these weight training exercises in your workout routine to build muscle, tone your body, and burn fat.

- **Squats:** Stand upright and bend your knees. Imagine sitting on a chair and bend your knees until your hamstrings are parallel to the floor. Do not let your knees go past your toe line.
- **Deadlifts:** This exercise strengthens your lower back. It is imperative to perform this exercise correctly. Performing with the wrong posture could damage your lower back, which is often irreversible.

- **Lunges:** Lunges target your quads, hamstrings, and hip muscles. Even though this exercise can be performed without weights, adding weights is a bonus.

- **Russian twists:** This exercise can be performed with and without weights. It increases your heart rate and targets all abdominal muscles. It also partly affects your arms and your back muscles.

- **Inverted rows:** This exercise targets your core, arms, shoulders, and back and is necessary to incorporate in your upper body workout. Just like deadlifts, it is necessary to focus on postures.

- **Push press:** Push press incorporates quarter squats in the exercise. This targets your arms, shoulders, chest, and hips.

You can buy weights and complete these exercises at home. However, joining a gym is ideal for weight training as it will help you stay consistent and provides you with the necessary equipment to achieve these vigorous exercises.

Duration: 60 minutes

Calories burned: 180 (for a 125-pound person)

Suitable for: Phase 2 of the diet

It's important to note that the number of calories burned in this given duration will vary from person to person. It depends on the individual's current weight (people who weigh more burn more calories as opposed to leaner individuals), their height, stamina, endurance, and medical conditions.

While incorporating some form of exercise is simpler for those who have exercised before or exercise regularly, it might seem like a challenge for the newbies. Focus on your diet during the first 2 weeks and add some form of exercise after this period. Ultimately, what form of exercise you choose boils down to the individual and how well they can incorporate the changes and make the most out of them.

Tweak Your Diet While Exercising

If you incorporate regular exercise daily in your weight loss regime, you might have to tweak your diet and eating habits to provide your body with enough nutrition. Since your body needs supplementary protein and calories to expend energy and build muscle, add to this, a low-calorie, healthy meal to your diet. Do not go overboard with calories as this hinders your progress, and you could gain more weight. Load up on protein after your workout as it helps build strength and accelerates the recovery process. As you may already know, more protein means more muscle build, and this means higher fat burning. Protein-rich food items such as soy and kale salad or turmeric chicken make great post-workout meals.

The Sirtfood Diet is a life-changing step that motivates you to eat healthily, exercise every day, and understand the importance of looking after your health. Once you incorporate this routine into your schedule, it will become a permanent part of your lifestyle. It might feel challenging and overwhelming initially and this is normal, but once you endure the first 2 weeks, the journey will seem a lot simpler. You will not want to go back to your old, less healthy lifestyle. Take it one step at a time and be patient.

Try to follow the Sirtfood Diet with your chosen exercise routine because they will help you lose weight and teach you healthy eating habits and how to sustain them for prolonged periods. In other words, this a great way to kick start a permanent fitness journey.

SECTION THREE: Meal Planning and Recipes

This part of the book talks about some practical aspects of this diet: meal planning and recipes. You will understand the importance of meal planning, how to do it, the types of ingredients you can use, and some sirtfood recipes you can follow throughout the 21 days and beyond.

Chapter 9: Shopping List

In this chapter, you will get a ready-made shopping list based on various grocery store sections. This will not only help you keep track of the groceries you need, but it will also make shopping easier. Take a printout of this list and get going.

Here's a shopping list for you to get started.

Fruits and Vegetables

- Kale
- Celery
- Spinach
- Apples
- Blueberries
- Strawberries
- Onions
- Garlic
- Ginger
- Arugula
- Parsley

- Coriander
- Tomatoes
- Avocados

Herbs and Spices

- Lovage
- Turmeric powder
- Cumin powder
- Curry powder
- Black pepper
- Bird's-eye chili
- Paprika
- Capers
- Red chicory

Dairy Products

- Cow or soy milk (or any other vegan milk of your choice)
- Butter
- Yogurt
- Grains and Legumes
- Buckwheat
- Rice (preferably brown)
- Rolled oats
- Soy

Condiments

- Low-fat mayonnaise
- Almond, walnut, or any other nut butter

Meat

- Chicken (breast and thighs)
- Fish (salmon or any other fish of your choice)
- Turkey

Miscellaneous

- Dark chocolate (85% or higher cocoa content)
- Red wine (Pinot noir)
- Walnuts
- Green tea or matcha green tea powder
- Coffee
- Eggs
- Extra virgin olive oil
- Medjool dates

This list has every sirtfood and other healthy elements needed for a successful journey.

However, before you begin your Sirtfood Diet, consider your pantry and scan it for items you may already have. This will show you what new recipes you can try in the meantime.

Some basic ingredients available in your pantry (that comply with the Sirtfood Diet), which are also readily available, include dairy products such as milk, lemons, and extra virgin olive oil. Some items may need to be bought from health stores or online.

Here are some of these ingredients:

Matcha green tea: This can be very difficult to find. The best place to get it is on Amazon. You will find plenty of sellers selling matcha green tea of various brands. If you find it too expensive, you can switch to traditional herbal tea with a little matcha (also available in grocery stores). However, it is highly recommended to try pure matcha green tea as it is packed with nutrients and amazing weight loss boosting properties. As mentioned, matcha green tea is the concentrated version of regular green tea leaves, which makes it at least five times more powerful. A small tub of matcha green tea powder costs from $15 to $30, and since you need only a small amount in your juice every day, it is totally worth it. Once you use this ingredient and notice results, you will not want to go back.

Coconut flakes and coconut milk: Even though coconut is not a part of the top 20 sirtfoods discussed earlier, it is still a healthy ingredient that can be incorporated into some recipes make curries and sauces. Coconut is rich in copper, manganese, iron, and some vitamins, which helps form red blood cells and promote bone health. It is also rich in selenium, which is needed to detoxify your cells and improve certain functions in your body. Since it is high in calories, resort to a few coconut flakes and coconut milk in your recipes. These two ingredients can usually be found in your local health shop or a nearby Asian grocery store. If not, buy a whole coconut.

Buckwheat noodles, pasta, and flakes: Since buckwheat is the main grain in the list of sirtfoods, it is essential to include it in your grocery list. Make buckwheat noodles or pasta for dinner or have buckwheat flakes for breakfast. Again, search for these ingredients in your local health shop. Some organic stores also sell buckwheat products. If not, look for it online. Know that these ingredients, especially the buckwheat flakes, might cost a fortune depending on where you live. If it is too expensive for your budget, you can stick to whole wheat pasta or brown rice, but to see the best results, try to include these ingredients in your meal plan. Since buckwheat is a sirtfood, it will push your results and boost your weight loss process.

Capers: Finding capers in local grocery stores any part of the world can be challenging. While capers are readily available in small jars in some countries, it can be very difficult to find almost everywhere. Look for a jar of capers by the olives and pickles. If it's not available, you may find it online. It can be expensive in some places, so, if it overshoots your budget, you can skip this ingredient (try not to, though).

Lovage: This fresh herb is another challenging item usually not found easily. It isn't even available online in some countries. Search for it in your local health store, grocery store or online. If you can't find it, you can skip this step.

Don't fret if you can't find all 20 sirtfoods. Stick to the ones you can easily find and the ones you will use in your meals frequently. Improvise and tweak your shopping list. However, it is highly recommended that you use at least ten of these sirtfoods to experience maximum results. Since some of these are commonly found in pantries, such as extra virgin olive oil, walnuts, and turmeric, you only have to look for the rest.

Making a Budget and Saving Money

Restrictive diets can be expensive, but only not if planned well. Since healthy ingredients are pricey, it's challenging to lose weight on a budget. If that's the case, simply follow these tips.

1. Add Only Essential Ingredients

Scan your pantry and list all the items you have. Now, consider the recipes and meals you are planning to cook. Add the ingredients you need and skip the ones you already have (you will learn more about this in the meal planning stage later in this book). Next, write the approximate quantity and cost of each ingredient you want to buy. If you don't know the price, look it up online. Calculate the total amount and add $20 to $25 to it, which will be your total budget. Set this amount aside every week and use only that money to buy your groceries.

Most important, stick to your list. It's very easy to get distracted in the grocery store and pick up things you don't really need. This bad habit can make you go over your budget, and you will end up spending more than you intended. One easy step to take is to avoid going shopping on an empty stomach. When you are hungry, you will be tempted to buy unhealthy items due to cravings. An easy way to go about this is to have eat a meal before you go shopping. Once you are full, you will not be so easily diverted by all the options you'll come across, which will make it easier to stick to your list.

2. Cook at Home

Avoid eating out and cook at home as often as you can. Even if you are ordering healthy food, it can cost 3 to 4 times more than what you can make at home. You'll want to set your budget as explained above; buy your ingredients and alternate between meals. You can find plenty of recipes online that teach you how to make restaurant-style food at home. If you stick to this plan, you will be saving money and making your meals healthier. The food you order can contain many harmful ingredients, some of which are processed, which can cause a significant backlash to your weight loss process or even reverse it. The same meal, when cooked at home, costs less, and is healthier and fresher. With this tip in mind, you will spare money and preserve your health from being compromised.

3. Buy Whole Foods and Generic Brands

Whole foods are generally cheaper and fresher as opposed to their processed and packaged counterparts. For instance, buying whole oats for breakfast compared to packaged cereal is healthier and much cheaper. It contains no additives, preservatives, or extra sugar, which will keep your health and energy levels in check. Similarly, a block of cheese costs less than shredded cheese. There is one catch here; you must buy the whole foods in bulk, which may initially seem to exceed your budget. This is because whole foods are available in larger quantities, and you cannot buy them for smaller servings. Even though it costs more initially, it saves you a lot in the long run. These larger quantities will sustain you for more than a month or 2 (depending on the number of members in your family), which will save you cash you can use on your next trip.

Further, you need to look for generic brands when buying a product. You can usually find generic brands in most stores for almost every food item. These are cheaper and adhere to the country's manufacturing and safety standards, making them safe for consumption. To ensure that the item meets the same quality as other expensive brands, check the ingredients on the packaging. While buying cheaper products can be a life saver, you also need to ensure its quality as it could otherwise slow down your weight loss process if it has a lot of additives.

4. Look for Offers, Sales, and Products in Season

Many grocery stores offer leaflets and put up advertisements on their websites when any offers, sales, or promotions come up. Keep an eye on these ads and stock up whenever any of your go-to ingredients are on sale. While stocking up fresh veggies is not advised, other ingredients with a longer shelf life such as buckwheat noodles and raw chickpeas can be bought in bulk and stored for a prolonged period. Buying ingredients on sale can save you a lot of money every trip you make to the grocery store, which can drastically cut costs.

Look for fresh products in season. Some local produce such as tomatoes, watermelon, or strawberries are fresher, cheaper, and readily available during their peak months. So, try to plan your meals around these ingredients as this will cost you less and provide optimum taste and freshness. It will also provide variety in your diet, which will make you want to stick to it for longer. Further, look for local produce in the farmer's market in your area. These are cheaper and fresher than the options you'll find in grocery stores. They do spoil quicker though, so try to consume them as soon as possible.

5. Buy Frozen Food

Last, go for frozen food such as berries, pineapple, mango, veggies, etc. These are cheaper than fresh fruits and vegetables and available all-year-round. Buying fresh ingredients during the off-season can cost 2 to 3 times more than the usual price. Frozen fruits and vegetables are equally nutritious as their fresh counterparts and can be bought in bulk. Further, you avoid waste by using the cut version of fruits and vegetables. Only use what you want and store it again in the freezer for further use; this will keep them fresh for a few months. You can make smoothies, cook curries with frozen them, or use them as a cereal topping.

As you can see, determining your budget and saving money on a restrictive diet aren't too difficult. Just stick to these tips to eat healthy on a budget.

Tools and Equipment Required

Aside from the basic ingredients you should always have in your pantry when on the Sirtfood Diet, you will also need basic tools and equipment to prepare your meals.

1. Juicer

The famous sirtfood green juice that needs to be consumed multiple times a day can be prepared helped by a juicer. Investing in a heavy-duty juicer is worth the price as it will allow you to prepare delicious smoothies with ingredients recommended on the Sirtfood Diet. The best machines for diets are usually available in three forms – centrifugal, citrus, and slow juicers. As the name suggests, citrus juicers are ideal for citrus fruits, such as oranges and lemons. But centrifugal and slow juicers are the best for vegetables and other fruits.

To make your green juice, go for a juicer easy to use, simple to clean, collects all the pulp in one place, provides quick results, and has the option of making bulk juices in one go.

2. Food Processor

Since this diet includes certain steps like chopping veggies, a food processor will make things easier. Leafy vegetables such as kale and arugula can be roughly chopped using this appliance. You can also prepare other healthy items in your diet with a food processor, such as cauliflower crust pizza, home-made peanut butter, oatmeal flour, mashed potatoes, or basil pesto. A food processor makes cooking easier and quicker and allows you to try a new variety of recipes and add it to your meal plan. It reduces the effort and food preparation is much more fun.

While selecting a food processor, check the blade power, bowl capacity, and body. It should accommodate more food, should be easy to assemble, and simple to clean and maintain.

3. Grilling Pan

Ingredients like chicken and fish need to be grilled in certain recipes such as turmeric and chicken curry or chicken skewers. Using a grill pan can make the process easier and saves a lot of time. You might already know this, but barbecued food can be healthy unless slathered with butter or marinated with unhealthy ingredients. Grilling and barbecuing your food is the easiest way to include tasty meals in your diet. Ingredients such as bell peppers, tofu, chicken, and tomatoes taste best when grilled. By adding only salt, you are also retaining the health and nutritional factor of these ingredients. If you are looking for some ideas for your next meal and want something delicious to eat, just place a few slices of veggies or chicken on the grill pan and serve with a bed of kale or rocket leaves and buckwheat.

To buy a high-quality pan, make sure that the size fits well within your designated cooking space. Second, it has to have a longer handle; this will make cooking safe and manageable. Also check the material of the pan. A cast-iron grilling pan is the best material for this purpose. Although it can be heavy, it keeps the food from sticking and retains heat to cook the food evenly, therefore producing excellent results.

Besides these, you should also have:

· A set of sharp knives

· Pots and pans

· Mixing bowls

· Measuring cups and spoons

· A chopping board

· A water bottle - to store drinking water and sip on it throughout the day

· A set of storage containers - to prepare and store your meals beforehand

· A mandolin or spiralizer - to grate or spiralize fruits and veggies for cooking or to add to salads

· A steamer basket - to steam your veggies

· A hand blender - to blend and thicken your sauces while they are cooking

While you might already have some of these tools in your home, you may have to invest in some essential items such as a juicer, a food processor, and a grilling pan. Do not hesitate to make these investments as you will reap a lot of benefits eventually.

Now that you have your shopping list and equipment tool list ready, it's time to visit the store and stock up.

Chapter 10: Meal Planner

This chapter will go through a step-by-step method to plan your meals and ways to organize and customize your Sirtfood Diet. We will also take a look at a 21-day meal plan to kick start your journey.

The term "meal planning" can sound overwhelming for newbies. Planning meals, learning recipes, buying groceries, counting calories and nutrients can be stressful when you're not used to them. Don't be discouraged though, it isn't as complicated as it sounds. This chapter will teach you ways to plan your meal and turn the process into a simple and menial task that can be carried out every week easily.

Before we begin, learn the exact definition and importance of meal planning. What is meal planning? And why is it necessary?

Meal planning refers to planning your breakfast, lunch, dinner meals, and snacks for a designated day or for the entire week. Your meal plan needs to abide by the calorie count allowed in your diet and should be balanced in nutrients. Basically, with meal planning, there is no longer the daily question of "What's for lunch?" Part of this journey is deciding on all the meals you plan to have for the next week. You'll also learn how important it is to shop for the ingredients and prepare them beforehand (if possible).

Now, let's consider a step-by-step approach to meal planning.

Step 1: Choose the Dishes or Recipes That Comply with the Guidelines of Your Diet

The Sirtfood Diet requires that you stick to a specific calorie counts for each week and include essential sirtfoods in your diet. To get ideas and recipes for some healthy and delicious sirtfood recipes, skip to the last chapter. Choose meals for your breakfast, lunch, and dinner, and scatter them across the week to stay versatile. Make sure that your choices adhere to the calorie count you're following.

To choose recipes on your own, don't just come up with one and hope for the best. Consider the meals you'll have before and after. Do they all adhere to the calorie count? Do they produce adequate nutrition for your lifestyle, depending on whether you're sedentary or active? Is it easy to prepare? Is it too time-consuming? Ask these questions before you decide on a recipe to venture with. You should also start prepping for the finalized recipes at least 3 days before. This way, you will have ample time to buy groceries and prep the ingredients.

Here's an easy way to choose your recipes based on the number of meals you'll have in the upcoming week: take a look at your calendar and mark the days you plan to have lunch and dinner at home. Let's say you are having five dinner meals in the coming week. Choose five dinner recipes and schedule them. Further, consider your schedule on the days you are cooking your meals. For instance, if you have to attend your kid's soccer practice in the evening, the best choice is to prepare your meal in a slow cooker. Transfer all the ingredients to your slow cooker and let it cook your meal for 8 to 10 hours. By the time you are home, it will be ready. If you're the individual who has to run errands throughout the day and doesn't have hours on end to spend in the kitchen, this will be your best option.

If you are cooking your meals, make extra. Use the leftovers for lunch the next day. Some minor adjustments and plans like these can make it easier for you to prepare your meals and stick to the plan.

Last, consider these four points to make choosing recipes easier:

A. Stick to the Recipe or Cooking Method You Know

Certain recipes like chicken turmeric curry or blueberry pancakes are common and are widely used in most households. The Sirtfood Diet allows certain recipes that are popular, which is why it would be simpler for you to incorporate these in your meal plan rather than looking for a less conventional recipe that you must learn from scratch. By choosing a familiar recipe you already know how to make, you'll also find it easy to gather the needed ingredients and to find the time required to prepare the dish. This will make it smoother for you to schedule your plan and stick to it.

B. Choose Recipes That Provide Leftovers

Leftovers are a boon for individuals with busy schedules. By making meals in bulk, you can store the leftovers for the next day. Simply warm them up and have them for lunch. If you don't feel like eating them as they are, just toss them in some olive oil and add some spices. Place them on a lettuce leaf or roll them with buckwheat or oat flour flatbread. You can always tweak them to make something interesting and delicious.

C. Cook Tempting Recipes

Some people erroneously believe that healthy meals cannot be tasty. This is simply not true. The Sirtfood Diet lets you cook meals that are healthy, nutritious, and incredibly delicious. Some recipes on this diet are probably tastier than your usual meals. The goal is to choose items that you'd look forward to and cannot wait to eat. So, stick to the recipes that you'd want to eat again.

D. Select Meals That Have Regular Ingredients

Finding and spending money on rare and exotic ingredients is not what anyone prefers. This either needs a lot of time or an expensive budget to accommodate these products. The safer bet is to stick to the regularly available ingredients, some of which should always be in your pantry. The Sirtfood Diet includes many items that can be abundantly found anywhere in the world, such as herbs and spices, which will make meal planning easy. You'll want to scan the ingredients already present in your cupboard and fridge. Think of all the healthy recipes that can include these ingredients. This will save you a lot of cash and avoid food waste.

Step 2: Buy All Necessary Ingredients Beforehand

Consider the recipes and the ingredients required for each meal. Prepare a list and buy them beforehand. Consider the grocery list mentioned in one of the earlier chapters and make yours. Stick to the list as it will keep you from buying more ingredients than you need.

Preparing a grocery list may seem like a tedious and time-consuming process. However, you can break this down into two simple steps:

Prepare a Master Ingredient List

While this won't be your main grocery list, it will help you formulate a decent, budget-friendly one. To prepare your master ingredient list, consider your chosen recipes, and jot down the things needed to prepare the meals. Now, consider the items in your pantry and fridge. Cross off what you already have, and by doing this you should be able to cross off most things on the list. Keep a handy master ingredient list with you and check it every week to know whether any components need to be restocked or not.

Prepare the Main Grocery Shopping List

It is now time to prepare the main grocery shopping list. Based on the ingredients left on the master ingredient list, categorize them into departments. But before you do that, list all the components needed for your recipes. Once you have the list, segregate the ingredients into groups so you can easily find them in your local shop. For instance, categorize all dairy products in one group and all fruits and veggies in another. This will not only help you keep track of your ingredients, but it will also make shopping in the store easier. This way, it will also be more challenging to forget an item.

For easier access, prepare a checklist and save it as you'll use it again in the upcoming weeks - print it and keep it in your pocket or purse for when you go shopping. You can also use checklist apps on your phone that allow you to cross off ingredients and give you reminders. One important thing to remember is to leave the frozen section for last; this is to keep things from defrosting or melting and making a mess in your grocery basket. Start with the meat section, swing by the dairy products, pick up all condiments and spices, followed by fruits and veggies, and last, make your way to the frozen section. Before you take off to the checkout, double-check the list according to your chosen recipes and make sure that you have everything.

Step 3: Prep the Ingredients and Meals

Last, assemble the ingredients you bought. Do any of your recipes require making a base or chopping veggies beforehand? If yes, prepare your ingredients and pack them in airtight containers to save time when cooking. Certain ingredients or steps like grilling chicken and peeling or chopping nuts can take a lot of time. Prepare these in bulk and use them as required. Try to make meals beforehand, too. By doing this, you will always have meals to feed on and save cooking time during the week.

If you work in an office at a 9-to-5 job, it must be difficult to cook all your meals and stick to a plan. All this hassle and stress will make you want to throw in the towel and grab anything accessible. On most days, you'll want to eat something you need not make for breakfast and lunch. This is where meal planning and prepping help you. You have a whole weekend to prepare your ingredients, base, and even some meals. All you require is an hour or two of your Sunday afternoon or evening.

Basic steps like peeling and chopping onions, garlic, vegetables, and herbs can be time-consuming. By doing these beforehand, you will save a lot of time when you cook. Other steps, like de-skinning the chicken or fish and grilling them beforehand also work.

Even though these steps seem simple, each one can be time-consuming. Failing to abide by the strategies throws a beginner off the track, which leads to failure, which is no wonder only a few manage to gain successful results.

Further, you need to stick to a meal plan approach that suits your needs, time, and budget. Just make sure that you follow the diet as you are supposed to; this is not a holy grail that needs to be followed strictly. Stick to what works for you and customize your program accordingly. The last thing you want is for all your efforts to go to waste. Meal planning helps you stay on track and makes your life simpler. Give yourself some room for experimentation and occasional cravings; it will make your meal plan more realistic and will encourage you to abide by it.

Take one step at a time and learn from your mistakes. Meal planning is an evolutionary process that can be tweaked and customized along the way. With a little practice, you can plan your meals with no hassles. Follow a method that works for you.

Common Misconceptions

With meal planning, beginners always assume the worst. These myths or fallacies can not only throw you off-guard but also keep you from trying any restrictive diet plan. Since what you eat is majorly responsible for weight loss, this could ruin your chances of burning fat and fitting into your summer dress.

Some common misconceptions regarding meals and meal planning include:

Myth #1: Meal Planning is Expensive

Everyone assumes that dieting is expensive. It sometimes is, but it mainly depends on the meals and recipes in your meal plan. Cut down on your frequent junk food takeaways and invest the money in green vegetables and other healthy ingredients that collectively cost the same or even less than your greasy food. To cut down the costs drive to the cheapest grocery store in your area and buy all ingredients in bulk; it will save you a lot of money in the long run. Budgeting is useful during dieting. Before you begin, allocate cash for groceries and meals, and stick to this budget every week. Once you begin, you will automatically cut down on alcohol, frequent takeaways, and desserts, which all costs more than your groceries if you think about it. Practice meal planning wisely, and you will save a lot in the long run.

Myth #2: Meal Planning is a Thick Binder

Meal planning is usually carried out for a week or two and kept in a notebook you can easily access. By planning your meals for a longer period (like one or two months), it is difficult to stick to it. While planning ahead is necessary, you should have a clear vision for only a week ahead. This will give you space to change your recipes in the long run, depending on your health, budget, and preferences. More important, put up your weekly meal plan in a place that is always visible or accessible, such as Google docs, your planner, or even a roughly drafted schedule stuck on your refrigerator.

Myth #3: Meal Planning is Only Suitable for Families or Couples

This is another myth that needs to be addressed. Meal planning is not only for families and couples. Although having a supportive partner or a family member is necessary to motivate you to follow a diet, you can also plan your meals and sustain the plan as an individual. Different strategies can be used by dieters with various strengths. If you are single or if you're planning to diet on your own, plan your meals. You should first choose recipes designed for only 1 or 2 people. Second, use leftovers for your meals the next day. By doing this, you stick to nutritious meals and save food from being thrown away. Last, prepare a base that can be used for most meals, such as grilled veggies or chicken breasts. This will save a lot of time and energy for individuals with busy schedules.

Myth #4: Meal Planning Includes Only Home-Cooked Food

Although your meals need to be home cooked, occasional takeaways and indulgences are not a huge deal if you rarely do it and if you stick to your calorie intake. Sticking to home only cooked meals can be discouraging. Your meal plan should have weekly cheat meals that allow you to indulge in your favorite dishes sometimes. This keeps your dieting journey intact, and you will find yourself rarely tempted to give in to cravings, but make sure these cheat meals are followed only once a week or every two weeks. Anything more than this can take a toll on your diet and reverse the results.

Myth #5: It Requires a Lot of Time and Is Inflexible

This is wrong. If done right, meal planning and prepping could save a lot of time and energy as opposed to cooking every day. Since you already know the meals and recipes beforehand, you can prepare your meals for the coming week whenever you have the time. If you have your lunch ready, you will stop looking around and stick to a healthy meal. Further, prepping your meals gives saves you time during the week, which can be utilized for productive activities. And meal prepping offers flexibility and offers room for experimentation and tweaks. When you stick to healthy recipes that comply with the diet guidelines and calorie count, revisions and customizations are allowed.

Addressing these myths is necessary as it will encourage you to begin dieting and follow your meal plan without feeling overwhelmed.

Next, let's take a look at what an actual meal plan looks like to help you start your diet.

21-Day Sirtfood Diet Meal Plan

Here is a 21-day meal plan you can follow to help you begin your fitness journey.

Week 1

The first seven days of your 21-day plan are the most crucial as these will majorly determine your success. Day 1, 2, and 3 need you to follow a 1,000-calorie plan with three green glasses of sirtfood juices distributed over the day and one meal (either for lunch or dinner).

Day 1 – Around 1,000 Calories

Early morning

A glass of warm water with fresh lemon juice

Breakfast

One glass of sirtfood green juice (you can see the recipe in the last chapter)

Lunch and dinner

One plate of prawn stir-fried with buckwheat noodles

One glass of sirtfood green juice (have this for dinner as the last meal of the day should be lighter than the lunch)

Mid-morning

One glass of sirtfood green juice

Evening - 2 pieces of dark chocolate (85% cocoa) or one square of dark chocolate with a small bowl of shelled edamame

Note: To enjoy the juices throughout the day, try to make a fresh glass before consumption. Do not prepare it beforehand as stale juices might cause digestive issues. However, fresh juices are nutrient-dense and taste better.

Day 2 - Around 1,000 Calories

Early morning

A glass of warm water with fresh lemon juice

Breakfast

One glass of sirtfood green juice

Lunch and dinner

One plate of kale and red onion dhal with buckwheat

One glass of sirtfood green juice (have this for dinner as the last meal of the day should be lighter than the lunch)

Snacks

Mid-morning

One glass of sirtfood green juice

Evening

Two pieces of dark chocolate (85% cocoa)

Day 3 - Around 1,000 Calories

Early morning

A glass of warm water with fresh lemon juice

Breakfast

One glass of sirtfood green juice

Lunch and dinner

One plate of chicken and kale curry with buckwheat

One glass of sirtfood green juice

Snacks

Mid-morning

One glass of sirtfood green juice

Evening

Two pieces of dark chocolate (85% cocoa)

Note: On the first 3 days of your diet, you can also add a small serving of shelled edamame or some extra protein with your snacks, such as egg whites or a small portion of grilled chicken. Make sure that your daily calorie count allows you to add these extra food options.

Day 4 - 1,500 Calories

Early morning

A glass of warm water with fresh lemon juice

Breakfast

Sirtfood muesli

Lunch and Dinner

Sirtfood chicken skewers with satay sauce

One glass of sirtfood green juice

Snacks

Mid-morning

One glass f sirtfood green juice

Evening

Two pieces of dark chocolate (85% cocoa)

Day 5 - 1,500 Calories

Early morning

A glass of warm water with fresh lemon juice

Breakfast

Sirtfood blueberry pancakes

Lunch and dinner

Sirtfood chickpea stew with baked potatoes

One glass of sirtfood green juice

Snacks

Mid-morning

One glass of sirtfood green juice

Evening

Two pieces of dark chocolate (85% cocoa)

Day 6 – 1,500 Calories

Early morning

A glass of warm water with fresh lemon juice

Breakfast

Sirtfood muesli

Lunch and dinner

One plate of prawn, stir-fried with buckwheat noodles

One glass of sirtfood green juice

Snacks

Mid-morning

One glass of sirtfood green juice

Evening

One sirtfood granola bar

Day 7 – 1,500 Calories

Early morning

A glass of warm water with fresh lemon juice

Breakfast

Date and walnut porridge

Lunch and dinner

One plate of prawn, stir-fried with buckwheat noodles

One glass of sirtfood green juice

Snacks

Mid-morning

One glass of sirtfood green juice

Evening

One cup of espresso, one bowl shelled edamame

Note: If you feel hungry between meals, add a small portion of shelled edamame, chicken, a hard-boiled egg, or a sirtfood granola bar that will sustain you through dinner.

During this week, you can either incorporate light exercises, such as walking and yoga or simply focus on the diet to avoid stress.

Week 2

Congratulations! You made it to week 2. Week 1 is usually the most difficult for beginners. Since it incorporates a major calorie restriction, some days can be too tough to endure. Keep thinking about the end results to stay motivated. From Day 8, you may drink a glass of wine every day or every alternate day.

Day 8 – Around 1,500 to 1,700 Calories

Early morning

A glass of warm water with fresh lemon juice

Breakfast

Sirtfood blueberry pancakes

Lunch and dinner

One plate of kale and red onion dhal with buckwheat

Baked salmon and mint salad

Snacks

Mid-morning

One glass of sirtfood green juice

Evening

One sirtfood granola bar

Day 9 - Around 1,500 to 1,700 Calories

Early morning

A glass of warm water with fresh lemon juice

Breakfast

A smoothie with frozen fruit and rolled oats with milk of your choice

Lunch and dinner

Sirtfood chickpea stew with baked potatoes

Sirtfood salad

Snacks

Mid-morning

One glass of sirtfood green juice

Evening

Two sirtfood bites

Day 10 - Around 1,500 to 1,700 Calories

Early morning

A glass of warm water with fresh lemon juice

Breakfast

Muesli, yogurt (or milk of your choice), and blueberries

Lunch and dinner

Turmeric, ginger, and kale curry

Strawberry buckwheat tabbouleh

Snacks

Mid-morning

One glass of sirtfood green juice

Evening

One square of dark chocolate and four walnut halves

Day 11 - Around 1,500 to 1,700 Calories

Early morning

A glass of warm water with fresh lemon juice

Breakfast

Walnut and date porridge topped with sliced strawberries

Lunch and dinner

Sirtfood chicken skewers with satay sauce

Prawn curry with buckwheat noodles

Snacks

Mid-morning

One glass of sirtfood green juice

Evening

Sliced strawberries, a handful of walnut halves

Day 12 - Around 1,500 to 1,700 Calories

Early morning

A glass of warm water with fresh lemon juice

Breakfast

Sirtfood shakshuka

Lunch and dinner

One plate of kale and red onion dhal with buckwheat

Baked salmon and mint salad

Snacks

Mid-morning

One glass of sirtfood green juice

Evening

A small bowl of shelled edamame, one square of dark chocolate

Day 13 - Around 1,500 to 1,700 Calories

Early morning

A glass of warm water with fresh lemon juice

Breakfast

Sirtfood blueberry pancakes

Lunch and dinner

Sirtfood chickpea stew with baked potatoes

Buckwheat dhal with kale

Snacks

Mid-morning

One glass of sirtfood green juice

Evening

Two sirtfood bites, one cup of coffee

Day 14 - Around 1,500 to 1,700 Calories

Early morning

A glass of warm water with fresh lemon juice

Breakfast

Berry smoothie

Lunch and dinner

Sirtfood chickpea stew with baked potatoes

Turmeric, ginger, and kale curry

Snacks

Mid-morning

One glass sirtfood green juice

Evening

One square of dark chocolate, a small bowl of blueberries

Week 3

Once you pass the first 2 weeks with success (which are also the two most important phases of the Sirtfood Diet), the journey becomes easier starting week 3. This is when you need to add exercises to boost weight loss and fitness results. It's best to incorporate basic exercises such as walking, jogging, yoga, and Pilates that don't require you to exert too much effort. The goal is to incorporate physical exercise every day for at least 30 to 60 minutes. Since you can also increase the calorie count, it is necessary to burn extra calories, which can be done by exercising.

Week 3 is also a part of Phase 2 of the Sirtfood Diet. You will need to follow the same calorie count as week 2 and tweak meals to introduce variety. Just like week 2, you will have three sirtfood balanced meals and one green juice every day.

Day 15 - Around 1,500 to 1,700 Calories

Early morning

A glass of warm water with fresh lemon juice

Breakfast

Muesli, yogurt (or milk of your choice), and blueberries

Lunch and dinner

Grilled chicken with buckwheat

Sirtfood salad

Snacks

Mid-morning

1 glass of sirtfood green juice

Evening

Celery sticks with hummus, one cup of coffee, a handful of walnuts

Day 16 - Around 1,500 to 1,700 Calories

Early morning

A glass of warm water with fresh lemon juice

Breakfast

Egg and mushroom scramble

Lunch and dinner

Tofu burgers with whole grain bread

Kale dhal with ginger

Snacks

Mid-morning

One glass of sirtfood green juice

Evening

One cup of coffee, 2 to 3 walnut halves, one square of dark chocolate (85% or higher)

Day 17 - Around 1,500 to 1,700 Calories

Early morning

A glass of warm water with fresh lemon juice

Breakfast

Sirtfood shakshuka

Lunch and dinner

One plate of kale and red onion dhal with buckwheat

Grilled chicken with satay sauce

Snacks

Mid-morning

One glass of sirtfood green juice

Evening

One cup of coffee, 2 to 3 walnut halves, ½ cup sliced strawberries

Day 18 - Around 1,500 to 1,700 Calories

Early morning

A glass of warm water with fresh lemon juice

Breakfast

A smoothie with frozen fruits and rolled oats with milk of your choice

Lunch and dinner

Rocket salad with tuna and tomatoes

Chicken turmeric curry with buckwheat

Snacks

Mid-morning

One glass of sirtfood green juice

Evening

A small bowl of shelled edamame, one sirtfood bite

Day 19 - Around 1,500 to 1,700 Calories

Early morning

A glass of warm water with fresh lemon juice

Breakfast

Kale omelet

Lunch and dinner

Kale salad with edamame beans and red onions

Buckwheat noodles with stir-fried prawns

Snacks

Mid-morning

One glass of sirtfood green juice

Evening

One sirtfood granola bar

Day 20 - Around 1,500 to 1,700 Calories

Early morning

A glass of warm water with fresh lemon juice

Breakfast

Walnut and date porridge with sliced strawberries

Lunch and dinner

Baked salmon and mint salad

Strawberry buckwheat tabbouleh

Snacks

Mid-morning

One glass of sirtfood green juice

Evening

A square of dark chocolate, one small bowl of blueberries, two walnut halves

Day 21 - Around 1,500 to 1,700 Calories

Early morning

A glass of warm water with fresh lemon juice

Breakfast

Egg and mushroom scramble

Lunch and dinner

Grilled fish with buckwheat

Ginger and kale curry

Snacks

Mid-morning

One glass of sirtfood green juice

Evening

One cup of espresso, two sirtfood bites

By the end of the 21st day, you will notice major changes in your body, mind, and behavior. You will feel more energetic, positive, and radiant. More important, you will see a major loss in body weight. Once you endure the 21 days, this diet will turn into a permanent lifestyle change. You will see why eating healthy is essential and what it does to your body. You may only regret not following it earlier. Some days, you may be tempted to give up and go back to your old habits. However, think about the amazing benefits you will gain by the end of this journey and think about the new, confident, radiant, and energetic lifestyle that you're following.

After the first two phases (first three weeks) of the Sirtfood Diet have passed, there are no specific rules for you to follow. You have only to keep on following the same diet, maintaining the calorie count, and integrating sirtfoods in your daily diet.

With the onset of week 4, incorporate exercises that expend more energy and burn more calories, such as HIIT, aerobics, and weight training. This will boost your weight loss results, provide you with more energy, and give your body a leaner and more toned look. Listen to your body and take it one step at a time. Also try to incorporate more rigorous exercises gradually.

Follow this 21-day plan to get started with your diet and body transformation. Some of these healthy sirtfood recipes are explained in more detail in the next chapter.

Chapter 11: Recipes

This is the time to learn some weight-loss friendly recipes that can be made quickly and incorporated into your daily meal plan. This chapter will provide 15 sirtfood recipes that can distributed over the two phases. Below are lunch, dinner, and snack recipes.

1. Sirtfood Green Juice

Since this juice is a recurring part of your diet, you need to master the recipe. The main ingredient is kale, and you can add arugula and parsley as needed. This juice is rich in nutrients and offers several health benefits. It boosts immune health, regulates digestion, and aids in weight loss, also making you feel lighter and more energetic. When consumed regularly the first few days of your diet, you'll notice an almost immediate change in our gut health, and you may find that your bowl movements are more frequent.

Serves: 1

Ingredients:

- 2.5 oz kale
- A handful of parsley
- 1 oz arugula
- 2 to 3 celery sticks
- ½ medium ginger root
- ½ lemon
- ½ medium green apple
- ½ tsp matcha green tea

- Drinking water as required

Directions:

1) Wash and chop the celery sticks into half. Peel the ginger and chop it roughly.

2) Add kale, parsley, arugula, celery sticks, ginger, and green apple in a juicer and blend it until all ingredients are mixed well. Add water to get the desired consistency if needed.

3) Transfer it to a glass. Squeeze fresh lemon juice and add matcha green tea, stir well and drink it immediately.

If you can't find the time to make a fresh batch every time, you can prepare this juice beforehand and store it in bulk. However, always add the lemon juice and matcha green tea only it is ready to be consumed to prevent the mixture from going bitter.

2. Walnut and Date Porridge

This is an interesting breakfast option that is equally nutritious and delicious. It uses walnuts, dates, and buckwheat as the main ingredients.

Serves: 1

Ingredients:

- 1.5 oz buckwheat flakes
- ½ cup milk (cow milk, soy milk, or almond milk)
- 1 Medjool date (roughly chopped)
- 1 tsp walnut butter
- Four walnut halves (roughly chopped)
- 3 to 4 strawberries (sliced)

Directions:

1) Heat milk in a pan and add the chopped Medjool date and mix well.

2) Once the milk is slightly hot, add the buckwheat flakes. Stir thoroughly until the date forms lumps.

3) Once the mixture reaches your desired consistency, take it off the flame and let it cool for a while.

4) Transfer it to a bowl and garnish with walnut butter, chopped walnuts, and sliced strawberries.

You can also add blueberries to this porridge. This recipe needs just a few ingredients and takes less than 10 minutes to prepare. Store these ingredients in your pantry to have a healthy and delicious breakfast option every morning.

3. Egg and Mushroom Scramble

If get bored with consuming the same sweet breakfast options given above, try this delicious breakfast recipe for a change.

Serves: 1

Ingredients:

- Two medium eggs
- 1 tsp extra virgin olive oil
- 0.75 oz kale (roughly chopped)
- ½ bird's-eye chili (finely chopped)
- 1.75 oz button mushrooms (cleaned and thinly sliced)
- 1 tsp turmeric powder
- 1 tsp curry powder
- A handful of parsley (finely chopped)
- Salt to taste
- Seed mixture of your choice (optional)
- Rooster sauce (for flavor, optional)

Directions:

1) Heat some oil in a pan and add the chili and thinly sliced mushrooms. Fry for a few minutes until the mushrooms turn golden brown. Set aside.

2) In a separate bowl, add turmeric powder and curry powder to the water and mix well to form a paste.

3) Meanwhile, heat some water in a pot and steam the kale until it is slightly cooked. It should take 2 to 3 minutes.

4) Heat more oil in the pan used to cook mushrooms and add the spice paste, eggs, salt, and the sauteed mushrooms. Mix well and let it cook for 1 to 2 minutes.

5) Add the steamed kale and mix well. Garnish it with chopped parsley and serve hot.

If you don't like mushrooms, you can skip this ingredient and use the eggs as the main ingredient. You can also substitute the mushrooms for any other healthy ingredient.

4. Sirtfood Salad

This salad is a filling meal that can be consumed for lunch or dinner. It contains salmon, capers, celery, arugula, avocado, and other healthy ingredients known to boost weight loss.

Serves: 1

Ingredients:

- 1.75 oz arugula leaves
- 1.75 oz endive leaves
- ½ cup avocado
- 3.5 oz salmon slices
- 1/6 cup red onion
- ½ cup celery
- A handful of walnut halves
- 1 Medjool date
- 1 tbsp capers
- 1 tsp fresh lemon juice
- ½ tbsp extra virgin olive oil
- ¼ cup parsley

- Salt to taste

Directions:

1) Wash and rinse the salad leaves to remove dirt. If it's not organic, it's best to wash them in a solution of water, vinegar and salt. Rinse well.

2) Chop the leaves into bite-sized pieces. Peel the avocado and chop it into tiny cubes.

3) Chop other ingredients, such as celery, red onions, and Medjool dates into slices.

4) Add all these ingredients in a bowl. Next, add the salmon slices, walnuts, and capers.

5) Add olive oil, salt, and lemon juice and mix well. Garnish with finely chopped parsley.

Salmon offers healthy fat and protein content, whereas the green leafy vegetable offers fiber and keeps you full for longer. However, all of these ingredients are low in calories. Avocado and olive oil also contribute to healthy fat content.

5. Prawn Stir-Fry with Buckwheat Noodles

You already know the benefits of using buckwheat as the main source of carb in the Sirtfood Diet. This is one of the many ways you can consume buckwheat in a delicious and nutritious meal of stir-fried prawns with noodles.

Serves: 1

Ingredients:

- 2.5 oz buckwheat noodles
- 5 oz raw prawns
- 2 garlic cloves
- 1 medium red onion
- 2 tbsp extra virgin olive oil
- 1 bird's-eye chili
- 2 tbsp tamari or soy sauce
- ½ ginger (grated)
- 1.75 oz kale
- 2.5 oz green beans

- 2 celery sticks
- ½ cup chicken stock

Directions:

1) Heat oil in a pan. Add some tamari to it.

2) Once the oil is heated, cook the prawns on both sides for around 2 to 3 minutes.

3) Place them on a plate and allow them to cool down at room temperature.

4) Meanwhile, add water to a pot and let it boil. Once the water bubbles, add noodles and let it cook for 6 to 8 minutes.

5) Heat some oil in the same pan used for cooking the prawns. Add garlic, ginger, red onion, chili, kale, beans, and celery and sauté them for a few minutes.

6) Once these ingredients are slightly fried, add some stock and mix well. Let it boil and simmer for a few minutes. Cook until the vegetables have softened.

7) When you're done, add the cooked prawns along with celery and cooked noodles to complete the recipe. Let them boil for a few more minutes and serve hot.

You can serve this dish as it is or with some extra soy sauce. Replace the soy sauce with tamari if you are avoiding gluten.

6. Strawberry Buckwheat Tabbouleh

This recipe is as interesting as it sounds. It uses the sweet and tangy flavor of strawberries and combines it with the nutty and earthy flavor of buckwheat - a delightfully delicious dish.

Serves: 1

Ingredients:

- ½ cup avocado
- 1 oz arugula
- 1/3 cup buckwheat
- 6 to 7 strawberries
- 1/6 cup red onion
- 1 medium tomato
- A handful of walnuts
- 1 Medjool date
- 1 tbsp turmeric powder
- 1 tbsp capers
- 1 tsp fresh lemon juice

- ½ tbsp extra virgin olive oil
- ¼ cup parsley
- Salt to taste

Directions:

1) Boil water in a pot, add turmeric, and cook the buckwheat for a few minutes. Drain the contents and let it cool for a while.

2) Wash and rinse the leafy greens in a solution of water, vinegar, and salt. Rinse well.

3) Chop the greens and other ingredients of tomatoes, strawberries, red onions, and Medjool dates into slices.

4) Add the buckwheat and the rest of the ingredients in a bowl.

5) Add olive oil, salt, and lemon juice, and mix well. Garnish with finely chopped parsley.

This dish will be a great addition to your lunch or dinner meal.

7. Sirtfood Blueberry Pancakes

This recipe is perfect for those with a sweet tooth. One popular sirtfood, blueberries, can be used in savory or sweet dishes. Pancakes are a breakfast staple and can be customized according to taste and needs.

Serves: 2

Ingredients:

- 8.5 oz blueberries
- 4 bananas
- 4 eggs
- 6.5 oz rolled oats
- 2 tsp baking powder
- Butter for frying
- Dark chocolate chips (optional)
- Salt, if required
- Water, if required

Directions:

1) First, start by preparing the oat flour. Transfer the rolled oats to a food processor and blend it well to turn it into a powdery or flour consistency. Ensure there is no moisture in your food processor as it could form lumps in your oat flour.

2) Add eggs, bananas, baking powder, and a pinch of salt to the food processor and blend it well until all ingredients are well-combined. You need the batter to be smooth and free of lumps.

3) Transfer it to a bowl and add blueberries. Carefully fold in the blueberries so the juice of the fruits remains intact. Let the mixture rest for 10 minutes.

4) Heat a pan and add some butter. Spread it evenly and pour a scoop of the pancake batter over it. Spread it to form an even circle according to the size you want.

5) Cook on both sides to achieve a golden-brown color.

You can also add some dark chocolate chips to the batter along with blueberries. These pancakes are a great addition to your usual breakfast routine. Serve it with some honey to enhance the taste. You can also replace the oats with buckwheat to adhere to the sirtfood guidelines.

8. Turmeric, Chicken, and Kale Curry

What's a better combination than turmeric, chicken, and kale? This curry, if prepared right, is a delicious dish that complies with the Sirtfood Diet guidelines. The earthy flavor of turmeric and kale combine with chicken's juicy texture to give you a healthy, nutritious, and sirtuin-rich meal. Pair it up with some rice or boiled buckwheat or enjoy it as it is.

Serves: 4

Ingredients:

- 14 oz chicken thighs (boneless)
- 7 oz kale
- 1 tbsp extra virgin olive oil
- 2 medium red onions
- ½ medium ginger root
- 3 to 4 garlic cloves
- 2 tbsp turmeric powder
- 2 bird's-eye chili (finely chopped)
- 1 tbsp curry powder

- 3 medium tomatoes
- 2 cardamom pods
- 1 cup chicken stock
- ½ cup coconut milk
- 2 cups water
- A handful of coriander leaves (for garnish)

Directions:

1) First, start by marinating the chicken. Transfer the skinless and boneless chicken thighs to a bowl and add turmeric. Massage it well for the chicken to absorb the marinade.

2) Heat oil in a pan and fry the chicken on both sides until it is well-cooked. Set it aside.

3) Heat more oil in the same pan and add chopped onions, garlic, bird's-eye chili, and grated ginger. Sauté it well until the onions turn golden brown.

4) Next, add some turmeric powder and curry powder and mix well. Let it cook for a few more minutes.

5) Add coconut milk, chopped tomatoes, cardamom pods, and chicken stock to the mixture and mix well. Pour in some water and let it simmer for a while. Keep stirring the mixture to avoid sticking or burning.

6) After 30 minutes, you will notice a reduction in the water level. Chop the kale and it them to the mixture. Stir well and let it simmer for a few more minutes.

7) After 5 to 10 minutes, add the cooked chicken pieces and mix well. Let it simmer again for a few more minutes until the chicken is warm.

8) Meanwhile, boil some water and cook rice or buckwheat to serve it with the kale and chicken curry.

Serve the curry with chopped coriander as garnish.

9. Baked Salmon and Mint Salad

Salmon and mint are other heavenly food combinations that complement each other perfectly. Use leafy greens, such as kale, arugula, and parsley for the base and top it off with a bed of baked salmon and mint dressing to complete the dish. This recipe is loaded with healthy fat and protein and is low in calories, making it an ideal addition to the Sirtfood Diet.

Serves: 1

Ingredients:

- 1.75 oz arugula
- 1.75 oz kale
- 3.5 oz salmon slices
- 1/6 cup red onion
- 2 medium radishes
- 1 small cucumber
- 1 tsp low-fat mayonnaise
- 1 tbsp yogurt
- A handful of mint leaves

- 1 tbsp rice vinegar
- ¼ cup parsley
- Salt to taste
- A pinch of black pepper

Directions:

1) Preheat the oven at 200 °C for 15 minutes. Once hot, place the salmon pieces in the oven and let them bake for 15 to 18 minutes until evenly cooked on both sides. For best results, remove the skin before baking.

2) While the fish is in the oven, wash and rinse the leafy greens in a solution of water, vinegar, and salt. Rinse well.

3) Chop the leafy greens, onions, cucumber, and radishes. Transfer all these ingredients into a bowl.

4) In a separate bowl, mix mayonnaise, yogurt, chopped mint leaves, rice vinegar, salt, and pepper. Mix well and let this sit for 10 minutes.

5) Take the serving bowl or plate and spread the leafy greens as the base. Add the chopped vegetables and mix them. Add the baked salmon and drizzle the mint dressing over it.

Garnish with finely chopped parsley and serve it for lunch or dinner.

10. Sirtfood Shakshuka

This is a new take on the traditional shakshuka recipe that most of us are familiar with. This recipe will substitute ingredients with sirtfoods such as bird's-eye chili, extra virgin olive oil, and red onions.

Serves: 1

Ingredients:

- 2 medium eggs
- 1 tbsp extra virgin olive oil
- 1 medium red onion
- 2 garlic cloves
- 1 tsp turmeric powder
- 2 bird's-eye chili (finely chopped)
- 1 tsp cumin powder
- 1 tsp paprika
- 1 oz kale
- 3 medium tomatoes
- Water (as required)
- 2 celery sticks

- A handful of parsley leaves (for garnish)

Directions:

1) Heat some oil in a pan and add chopped red onions and minced garlic cloves. Fry until the onions turn golden brown.

2) Add cumin powder, paprika, bird's-eye chili, turmeric powder, and chopped celery. Mix well and let the mixture cook for a few minutes.

3) Add chopped tomatoes and mix well. Add some water as required and let it simmer on low flame.

4) Chop the kale and add them to the mixture. Let it cook for a few more minutes.

5) Once the sauce is cooked, make 2 wells and pour in the eggs. Do not mix the eggs with the sauce.

6) Cover the pan with a lid and let it cook for 10 minutes on a low flame. Once the egg whites are firm and the yolks are runny, turn off the flame and let it sit with the lid for a few minutes.

7) Transfer the sauce and eggs to a plate and garnish with chopped parsley.

You can eat this meal as it is or serve it with some buckwheat or rice as a side. This dish is versatile and can be easily tweaked so you can have it for breakfast, lunch, or dinner.

11. Dark Chocolate Granola Bars

Do you ever crave a delicious snack while on a strict diet? Look no further. This tasty and healthy version of granola is a pantry essential. It satiates your sweet tooth and makes for a healthy snack post-lunch. You don't have to rely on the heavily processed granola bars sold commercially. However, dark chocolate chips are rich in sirtuin-activating nutrients and offer several health benefits. In this recipe, you will also add oats, pecans (or walnuts), and a dash of olive oil.

Serves: 8

Ingredients:

- 7 oz rolled oats
- 2 oz dark chocolate chips (75% or 85% cocoa)
- 1.5 oz pecans or walnuts
- 2 tbsp rice malt syrup
- 1 tbsp dark brown sugar
- 0.7 oz butter
- 2.5 tbsp olive oil

Directions:

1) Roughly chop the pecans or walnuts and transfer them to a bowl. Add rolled oats and mix well.

2) Heat some butter in a pan. Add brown sugar, rice malt syrup, and olive oil. Mix well until the ingredients are well blended. Make sure that the mixture doesn't boil.

3) Once the syrup has cooled down to room temperature, add it to the oats and walnuts. Mix well until the oats and walnuts are fully covered in the syrup.

4) Meanwhile, preheat the oven at 160 °C for 10 to 15 minutes. Line parchment paper on a baking tray.

5) Shape the oats mixture evenly over the baking tray. Bake for 20 minutes until both sides are golden brown.

6) Let them cool for a few hours. Once they have reached room temperature, break the bigger lumps and coat them with dark chocolate chips.

7) Cut them into bars and store them in airtight containers. You can use these for up to 2 weeks.

Prepare these granola bars in bulk to always have them handy whenever you crave something sweet. Double the ingredients if you want a bigger batch of granola bars. By wrapping these bars in wax paper and refrigerating them, you can use them for 1 or 2 months or also prepare them for your friends and family. To use them for over 2 months, freeze these bars and defrost at room temperature for 12 to 24 Hours.

12. Chicken Skewers with Satay Sauce

This appetizer can also be customized into a fulfilling meal with some modifications. Just add some buckwheat or rice as a side dish to have it for lunch. In this recipe, you will be using the classic combination of turmeric and chicken along with other sirtfoods, such as celery, red onions, walnuts, extra virgin olive oil, and buckwheat.

Serves: 1

Ingredients:

- 5 oz chicken breast (chopped)
- 1 oz kale
- 1 tbsp extra virgin olive oil
- 1 medium red onion
- 4 walnut halves
- 2 garlic cloves
- 2 tbsp turmeric powder
- 1 tbsp curry powder
- 2 celery sticks

- ½ cup chicken stock
- ½ cup coconut milk
- 1 tbsp walnut butter (or any other nut butter available)
- 1.75 oz buckwheat
- 1 cup water
- A handful of coriander leaves (for garnish)

Directions:

1) To marinate the chicken, transfer it to a bowl and add turmeric powder and olive oil. Massage it well for better absorption of the marinade. Cover the bowl and let it sit for 30 to 60 minutes.

2) Heat some olive oil in a pan. Add onions and garlic. Fry until the onions turn golden brown.

3) Add turmeric powder and curry powder. Mix well and let it cook for 2 to 3 minutes.

4) Next, add coconut milk and chicken stock to the mixture and mix well. After a few minutes, add walnut butter and mix until it is all well blended. Pour in some water and let it simmer for a while. Keep stirring the mixture.

5) After simmering it on a low flame for 10 minutes, you will notice a reduction in the water level, and the mixture will turn creamy.

6) Meanwhile, boil some water and cook rice or buckwheat to serve it with chicken skewers. Add chopped kale and celery to the buckwheat.

7) Prepare the skewers by threading the marinated chicken pieces over it. Grill the chicken until they are golden brown.

8) Transfer the grilled chicken pieces to a plate and pour in the cream satay sauce.

Serve the curry with chopped coriander as garnish. Roughly chop the walnut pieces and sprinkle over the chicken. If buckwheat isn't available, you can serve the grilled chicken with rice or enjoy it as an appetizer.

13. Sirtfood Bites

This interesting snack recipe is perfect for desserts or as an evening snack with a cup of espresso or green tea. These bites are made of popular sirtfoods, which are walnuts, olive oil, Medjool dates, turmeric, and dark chocolate. You can also call them healthy sirtfood truffles.

Serves: 15 to 18 bites

Ingredients:

- 8.75 oz Medjool dates
- 4.25 oz walnuts
- 1 oz dark chocolate (85% cocoa)
- 1 tbsp turmeric powder
- 1 tbsp dark cocoa powder
- 1 tbsp extra virgin olive oil
- 1 tsp vanilla extract
- 2 tbsp water

Directions:

1) Roughly chop the walnuts and dark chocolate pieces into tiny nibs.

2) Pit the Medjool dates and chop them into tiny pieces.

3) Add the broken chocolate and walnut pieces to a food processor and blend until they form a fine powder.

4) Transfer the mixture to a bowl and add the chopped Medjool dates, dark cocoa powder, olive oil, and turmeric powder. Mix well until all ingredients are combined well. Use a food processor to mix them thoroughly.

5) If needed, add some water for a more uniform consistency. However, you don't want the mixture to be too sticky.

6) Apply 1 or 2 drops of olive oil on your palms and spread the batter evenly. Take a part of the mixture and roll it into a ball between your palms.

7) Once all the mixture is used, and the balls are rolled, refrigerate them for 45 to 60 minutes.

For an additional touch, roll the balls over cocoa powder or desiccated coconut to enhance the taste. If refrigerated, these sirtfood bites can be used for up to a week. You can also prepare them in bulk and freeze them to store them for longer.

14. Sirtfood Chickpea Stew with Baked Potatoes

This is something you can find the time to prepare every once in a while. This recipe is delicious, nutritious, and incredibly filling.

Serves: 4 to 6

Ingredients:

- 2 cans chickpeas (pre-boiled, 400 grams each)
- 1 tbsp extra virgin olive oil
- 2 medium red onions (finely chopped)
- 2 garlic cloves (peeled and halved)
- 1 medium ginger root (peeled and grated)
- 4 to 6 potatoes
- 2 tsp chili flakes
- 2 bird's-eye chili (finely chopped)
- 2 medium tomatoes (chopped)
- 2 tbsp unsweetened cocoa powder
- 2 yellow peppers (chopped)
- 2 tbsp turmeric powder

- 1 tbsp cumin seeds
- 1 cup water
- Salt and pepper to taste
- A handful of parsley leaves (finely chopped, for garnish)

Directions:

1) Heat some oil in a pan and sauté the red onions until they turn brown.

2) Add garlic cloves, ginger, bird's-eye chili, chili flakes, and cumin seeds, and mix well. You can skip the chili flakes if you don't want it to be too spicy.

3) Once the spices are cooked, add turmeric powder and some water. Mix well and let them simmer on a low flame for a few minutes. Do not turn the flame high as it could burn the spices.

4) Meanwhile, preheat the oven to 200 °C. Once it's hot, line a baking tray and bake the potatoes for an hour.

5) Add tomatoes, yellow peppers, cocoa powder, and chickpeas to the pan with the spices and mix well. Add some water and close the pan with a lid. Let them simmer until the mixture boils.

6) The sauce should be ready within 45 minutes. Once it is thick and smells good, add salt and pepper and stir well.

Serve with chopped parsley as a garnish and a baked potato as a side dish. You can skip baking potatoes, replace them with buckwheat, and serve the dish as a curry. This recipe, if mastered, will be one of your favorites.

15. Kale and Red Onion Dhal with Buckwheat

This recipe is a sirtfood staple. It is delicious, easy to make, and highly nutritious. If you are looking for a recipe that is gluten-free and vegan, this is your go-to.

Serves: 4

Ingredients:

- 3.5 oz kale (or spinach)
- 5.25 oz red lentils
- 1 tbsp extra virgin olive oil
- 1 medium red onion (finely chopped)
- 2 garlic cloves
- ½ medium ginger root (peeled and grated)
- 2 bird's-eye chili (finely chopped)
- 2 tsp turmeric powder
- 1 tbsp curry powder or garam masala
- ½ cup coconut milk
- 1.75 oz buckwheat

- 1 cup water
- A handful of parsley or coriander leaves (for garnish)

Directions:

1) Heat some oil in a pan and sauté the red onions until they turn brown.

2) Add garlic cloves, ginger, and bird's-eye chili, and mix well.

3) Once the spices are cooked, add turmeric powder, curry powder, and some water. Mix well and let them simmer on a low flame for a few minutes. Do not turn the flame high as this could burn the spices.

4) Next, add coconut milk, red lentils, and some water. Stir well. Add some water and close the pan with a lid. Let it simmer until it boils. If the dhal turns too thick or sticks to the bottom of the pan, add more water and keep stirring the mixture.

5) Last, add chopped kale and mix it within the dhal. Close the pan with a lid and let it cook for 5 more minutes.

6) In a separate pot, boil some water and cook buckwheat for 10 to 15 minutes to serve it with the dhal.

Serve the dhal with chopped parsley as a garnish and cooked buckwheat as a side. Since the ingredients for this recipe are readily available, it is super easy to make, and you can make it a staple dish in your diet.

These recipes adhere to the Sirtfood Diet guidelines and offer a myriad of health benefits besides weight loss. The Sirtfood Diet is simply based on healthy eating, and these recipes are just perfect for kick starting your journey.

Conclusion

That sums up everything you need to know about the Sirtfood diet, now it's time to get started! The Sirtfood Diet is a long-term nutrition plan that should be followed for a prolonged period and incorporated into your lifestyle. Since this diet allows regular foods and some indulgences, it is easier to follow it for a long time than other diets. If you feel that the diet is too overwhelming due to major calorie restrictions in the first week, consume a moderate number of calories while sticking to the recommended sirtfoods. However, the side effects like light-headedness and nausea will pass away after the first week. So, try to follow the first 3 days with a 1000-calorie intake to achieve the best results.

Since the Sirtfood Diet's main goal is healthy eating and not weight loss, follow it for the long term. The first 21 days act as a kick-starter to begin your fitness journey and help you switch to healthy eating. So, continue this diet even after the first 21 days. By the end of 21st day, you should have a clear idea about the type of meals you'll have. Figuring out the number of calories and nutrients consumed in a day is also essential. To sustain it for longer, prepare your recipes with the top 10 or 20 sirtfoods. Also, have at least 1 glass of green juice every day, not only for weight loss but also to boost other crucial body functions. Remember this diet plan is meant to be implemented for the rest of your life and not only for 21 days.

Make sure that you do not have any underlying issues, as explained earlier. People with diabetes, an active lifestyle, or those with medical conditions shouldn't follow this diet. If you have questions about your body type and its effect on the Sirtfood Diet, consult your physician before you follow this diet.

It is now time to start your weight loss journey with the Sirtfood Diet and witness a new you. Try these recipes and meal plans today to lose weight. The Sirtfood Diet will not only give you a fitter and well-toned body but a new outlook to life and elevated self-confidence. Good luck!

Part 2: Sirtfood Recipes

A Cookbook with 100+ Recipes for Making the Most of the Sirtfood Diet

Introduction

If you are looking for a diet that helps attain your weight loss and fitness objectives without compromising your taste buds, try the Sirtfood diet. It teaches healthy eating habits and increases your body's natural metabolism by activating a group of proteins known as sirtuins.

The Sirtfood diet was created by the famous duo of health consultants and celebrity nutritionists Aidan Goggins and Glen Matten. Instead of purely concentrating on weight loss, this diet encourages healthy eating patterns. The secret to weight loss and enhancing your body's natural mechanism and its healing powers is to consume foods rich in sirtuins. This is not a fad diet; it activates your body's natural fat-burning mechanism, promoting weight loss, enhancing your immune function, is incredibly simple to follow, and leaves you feeling energetic. A great thing about this diet is that you can achieve all the benefits it offers without depriving yourself of the foods you enjoy. TV chef Lorraine Pascal, model Jodie Kidd, champion boxer David Haye, and beloved music icon Adele follow the Sirtfood diet. From red wine and dark chocolate to coffee, you can add different delicious ingredients to this diet.

In this book you will learn about the Sirtfood Diet, the benefits it offers, and sirtuin-rich foods. You will discover simple and practical tips to get started with this diet, meal planning, and a 4-week meal plan. Once you understand this diet's basics, it is time to follow the simple advice in this book. Besides this, you will discover several Sirtfood diet recipes. The recipes are classified into different categories for your convenience, such as breakfast, lunch, snacks, dinner, dessert recipes, etc. Remember: following this diet is extremely simple. Ensure that you stick to this protocol for at least four weeks to see a positive change in your overall physical wellbeing.

If you are excited to learn more about this diet and discover its weight loss and health benefits, then let's get started right away.

SECTION ONE: Sirtfood Diet Basics

Chapter 1: What is The Sirtfood Diet?

The Sirtfood diet was developed by a duo of celebrity nutritionists Aidan Goggins and Glen Matten. It's surprising to note that they managed to develop this diet while working in a private gym. This diet concentrates on the consumption of foods rich in sirtuins. *Sirtuins* is the term used to describe supercharged proteins found in the body that regulate various functions such as metabolism, inflammation, and immunity. This duo discovered that certain plant compounds increase levels of certain proteins known as *Sirt* foods. Combining the basic protocol of calorie restriction and increasing consumption of Sirt foods increases the production of sirtuins.

The duo stresses this diet isn't a fad diet. Sirt food is the key to unlocking the body's natural fat loss and healing mechanism. This diet has successfully managed the world of health and fitness. Did you know that the secret to Adele's stunning weight loss is the Sirtfood diet? So, if you are struggling to drop those excess pounds or wish to improve your overall health, this diet is a great idea.

The Sirtfood diet was originally created to overcome the basic challenges of fasting while reaping all its benefits. Fasting promotes weight loss, stabilizes blood sugar levels, increases fat loss, and strengthens the immune system. However, fasting isn't sustainable in the long run, is difficult to follow, is extremely restrictive, increases the risk of malnourishment, and results in muscle loss. The Sirtfood diet replicates the health benefits of fasting without its drawbacks.

Goggins and Matten believe this diet works by activating the *skinny gene*. While developing the Sirtfood diet, they conducted a study at their fitness center in the UK with 39 participants who followed the Sirtfood diet and exercise regularly for a week. The duo published their surprising results in their book "EAT YOUR WAY TO RAPID WEIGHT LOSS AND A LONGER LIFE BY TRIGGERING THE METABOLIC SUPERPOWERS OF THE SIRTFOOD DIET." The authors noted that the participants lost an average of seven pounds at the end of the first week. They also noted that certain participants gained lean muscle mass.

The weight loss was associated with the conscious deprivation of glycogen. Your body uses glycogen to supply the energy required to keep going and maintain its overall functioning. When the energy levels decline, the body uses the additional stores of glycogen present within. Once these stores are empty, it uses fats to produce the energy required. One molecule of glycogen is stored with four molecules of water. So, when your body's glycogen stores are depleted, all the water stored within it is also expelled. So, the initial weight loss (the first week or so) is due to the reduction of water weight and the glycogen stored within.

Once your calorie intake increases, your body replenishes the lost glycogen reserves. This is the reason the Sirtfood diet prescribes healthy calorie restriction. By increasing your sirtuin-rich food intake, you give your body all the nutrients it needs without the unnecessary calories. This diet is about eating smart instead of eating less.

Sirtuin Foods

Here's a list of the best Sirt foods you should add to your daily diet.

- Red wine
- Coffee
- Dark chocolate (85% cocoa content)
- Onions
- Strawberries
- Blueberries
- Kale
- Soy
- Parsley
- Extra virgin olive oil
- Arugula
- Chili
- Matcha green tea
- Walnuts
- Turmeric
- Buckwheat
- Medjool dates
- Chicory
- Lovage
- Capers

Chapter 2: How to Follow the Sirtfood Diet

The Sirtfood diet is divided into two phases. You need to follow specific instructions in each phase because they help change your body's overall metabolism. Phase 1 and 2 of this diet lasts for three weeks altogether. After this, you must follow the diet for longer to attain your weight loss and fitness objectives.

Phase 1

During phase 1 of this diet, your calorie intake is reduced to 1000 calories per day. It is also known as the hyper-success stage and lasts for one week. The seven days are further divided into two segments. During the first three days of the diet, your calorie intake is 1000 calories per day. After that, your calorie intake increases to 1500 calories per day. You need to drink three Sirtfood green juices and eat one meal per day within the allocated 1000 calories. After the three-day period, you can consume two Sirtfood diet meals and drink two juices within the 1500-calorie limit.

Phase 2

Once you have completed the phase-1 of this diet, don't forget to congratulate yourself! Phase 1 is perhaps the toughest part of this diet; once completed, the rest becomes easier. Phase 2 of this diet is also known as the maintenance stage, and its primary goal is to ensure that all the benefits derived during the previous stage are maintained. Don't worry about consuming juices instead of meals during this period. During the maintenance period, you can consume three wholesome Sirtfood meals and one Sirtfood juice. This phase lasts for two weeks. By increasing the consumption of such superfoods, you can easily maintain your body's nutrient requirements.'

Once you have completed a cycle of phases 1 and 2 of the Sirtfood diet, you need to repeat the process again. Since this diet is sustainable in the long run, ensure you consume healthy and well-balanced meals. A major advantage of this diet is the overall flexibility it offers. To enhance this diet's benefits, don't forget to add sufficient exercise to your daily routine. Diet, sleep, and exercise are three important factors essential for your overall wellbeing. So, pay attention to them!

As with any other diet, creating a plan is quintessential. It is not just about losing weight, but you need to maintain that weight loss and work towards your fitness goals. After three weeks, if you give up and go back to your unhealthy eating patterns, it will effectively undo all the Sirtfood diet's results thus far. To make things easier, use the four-week Sirtfood diet meal plan discussed in this book.

SECTION TWO: Sirtfood Recipes

Chapter 3: Beverages

Green Juice #1

Preparation time: 10 minutes

Cooking time: 0 minutes

Number of servings: 2

Ingredients:

- 4 large handfuls kale leaves, torn
- A handful flat-leaf parsley
- A handful lovage leaves
- 2 large handfuls rocket
- 1 medium green apple, cored, sliced
- 1 teaspoon matcha green tea powder
- Juice of a lemon
- 6 celery sticks with leaves, chopped

Directions:

1. Add kale, parsley, lovage, rocket, apple and celery into a juicer and extract the juice.

2. Add lemon juice and stir.

3. Matcha green tea powder is to be stirred in just before serving.

4. Pour into 2 glasses and serve with ice.

Green Juice # 2

Preparation time: 5 minutes

Cooking time: 0 minutes

Number of servings: 2

Ingredients:

- 5.3 ounces kale leaves, torn
- A small handful parsley
- 1 green apple, cored, sliced
- Juice of a lemon
- 2 handfuls rocket lettuce
- 4 celery sticks, chopped
- 1 inch ginger, sliced
- 1 teaspoon matcha green tea powder

Directions:

1. Add kale, parsley lettuce, ginger, apple and celery into a juicer and extract the juice.
2. Add lemon juice and stir.
3. Matcha green tea powder is to be stirred in just before serving.
4. Pour into 2 glasses and serve with ice.

Green Juice # 3

Preparation time: 10 minutes

Cooking time: 0 minutes

Number of servings: 1

Ingredients:

- 1 cup packed baby spinach leaves
- 2 cups packed baby kale leaves
- A small handful parsley
- 1 small cucumber, chopped
- Juice of ½ lemon

- ½ medium green apple, cored
- ½ inch fresh ginger, sliced

Directions:

1. Add kale, parsley, ginger, spinach, apple and cucumber into a juicer and extract the juice.
2. Add lemon juice and stir.
3. Pour into a glass and serve with ice.

Kale and Celery Juice

Preparation time: 5 minutes

Cooking time: 0 minutes

Number of servings: 2

Ingredients:

- 10 large kale leaves, torn
- 2 cucumbers, trimmed, chopped into chunks
- ½ cup pineapple chunks
- 3 – 4 large celery stalks, chopped

Directions:

1. Add kale, cucumbers, pineapple and celery into a juicer and extract the juice. If you are using fresh pineapple, consume the juice within 30 minutes of juicing.
2. Pour into 2 glasses and serve with ice.

Parsley Juice with Ginger and Apple

Preparation time: 5 minutes

Cooking time: 0 minutes

Number of servings: 2

Ingredients:

- 5 ounces parsley, stem and leaves
- 2 tablespoons honey
- 2 green apples, cored, sliced

- A handful fresh mint leaves
- 2 inches ginger, sliced

Directions:

1. Add parsley, ginger, apples and mint leaves into a juicer and extract the juice.
2. Add honey and stir.
3. Pour into 2 glasses and serve.

The Green Machine

Preparation time: 15 minutes

Cooking time: 0 minutes

Number of servings: 2

Ingredients:

- 2 inches fresh ginger, sliced
- 2 cucumbers, trimmed, chopped
- Juice of a lime
- Juice of a lemon
- 2 cups coconut water
- 2 cups baby kale leaves
- 2 very large chard leaves, torn
- 2 stalks celery, chopped
- 2 apples, cored, sliced
- 2 cups packed arugula

Directions:

1. Squeeze out juice from lime and lemon.
2. Add apples, ginger, kale, chard, arugula, and cucumber and extract the juice.
3. Stir in the coconut water, lime and lemon juice.
4. Pour into 2 glasses.
5. Add ice if desired and serve right away.

Savory Kale and Tomato Juice

Preparation time: 10 minutes

Cooking time: 0 minutes

Number of servings: 2

Ingredients:

- 6 medium plum tomatoes, chopped into chunks
- 4 stalks celery, chopped
- Juice of a large lemon
- 2 cups flat-leaf parsley
- 6 kale leaves, torn
- 2 tablespoons chia seeds (optional)

Directions:

1. Add tomatoes and parsley into the juicer first followed by celery and kale. Extract the juice and stir in the lemon juice and chia seeds.
2. Let it rest for 5 minutes.
3. Pour into 2 glasses and serve.

Grape and Melon Juice

Preparation time: 10 minutes

Cooking time: 0 minutes

Number of servings: 2

Ingredients:

- 1 cucumber, trimmed, chopped
- 7 ounces red seedless grapes
- 2 handfuls baby spinach
- 7 ounces cantaloupe, peeled, deseeded, chopped

Directions:

1. Add cucumber, grapes, spinach and cantaloupe into a juicer and extract the juice.
2. Pour into 2 glasses and serve.

Kale and Black Currant Smoothie

Preparation time: 5 minutes

Cooking time: 0 minutes

Number of servings: 1

Ingredients:

- 1 teaspoon honey
- 5 baby kale leaves, discard stalks
- A handful black currants, discard stalks
- ½ cup freshly brewed warm green tea
- ½ banana, sliced
- Ice cubes, as required

Directions:

1. Add honey into the cup of green tea. Stir and pour into a blender.
2. Add kale, currants, banana and ice cubes.
3. Blitz for 30 – 40 seconds or until smooth.
4. Pour into 2 glasses and serve.

Strawberry Smoothie

Preparation time: 10 minutes

Cooking time: 0 minutes

Number of servings: 2

Ingredients:

- 1 cup frozen strawberries
- 2 tablespoons brown rice protein powder
- 4 medjool dates, pitted, soaked in water for 20 minutes, drained, chopped
- 1 teaspoon grated fresh ginger
- Stevia to taste
- 4 stalks celery, chopped
- 2/3 cup coconut milk
- 4 tablespoons dark cocoa powder

- 2 tablespoon coconut palm sugar
- 1 cup green tea, cooled

Directions:

1. Add strawberries, protein powder, dates, ginger, stevia, celery, coconut milk, cocoa powder, coconut palm sugar and green tea into a blender.
2. Blitz for 30 - 40 seconds or until smooth.
3. Pour into 2 glasses and serve.

Mixed Berry Smoothie

Preparation time: 10 minutes

Cooking time: 0 minutes

Number of servings: 2

Ingredients:

- 2 cups mixed frozen strawberries, blueberries raspberries and blackberries
- 2 - 4 tablespoons cashew butter
- 1 ½ cups milk of your choice
- 2 tablespoons chia seeds
- 2 bananas, sliced, frozen

Directions:

1. Add strawberries, cashew butter, milk, chia seeds and bananas into a blender.
2. Blitz for 30 - 40 seconds or until smooth.
3. Pour into 2 glasses and serve.

Chocolate Smoothie

Preparation time: 10 minutes

Cooking time: 0 minutes

Number of servings: 2

Ingredients:

- 2 bananas, sliced, frozen
- 6 - 8 dates, pitted
- 1 ½ cups unsweetened almond milk of your choice
- 2 tablespoons unsweetened cocoa powder

Directions:

1 Add milk, cocoa and dates into a blender and blitz until smooth.
2 Add banana and blitz until smooth.
3 Pour into glasses and serve.

Apple Pie Smoothie

Preparation time: 60 minutes

Cooking time: 3 minutes

Number of servings: 3 - 4

Ingredients:

- 1 cup rolled oats
- 2 teaspoons vanilla extract
- 1 cup ice cubes
- 2 apples, cored, peeled, chopped into chunks
- 1 cup Greek yogurt
- 1 cup green tea

Directions:

1. Follow the directions on the package and brew the green tea. Chill for 50 - 60 minutes.
2. Pour into a blender. Add oats, vanilla, ice, apple and yogurt.
3. Blitz for 30 - 40 seconds or until smooth.
4. Pour into 2 glasses and serve.

Blueberry Pie Smoothie

Preparation time: 5 minutes

Cooking time: 0 minutes

Number of servings: 1

Ingredients:

- ¼ teaspoon ground cinnamon
- ¼ teaspoon grated lemon zest
- ¾ cup frozen blueberries
- ¼ cup coconut milk
- ½ teaspoon collagen powder
- Water, as required

Directions:

1. Add blueberries, coconut milk and lemon zest into a blender.
2. Blitz for 30 - 40 seconds or until smooth.
3. Add water if required and collagen powder. Pulse for 4 - 5 seconds.
4. Pour into a glass and serve.

Berry & Green Tea Smoothie

Preparation time: 60 minutes

Cooking time: 0 minutes

Number of servings: 3 - 4

Ingredients:

- ½ cup strawberries
- ½ cup blueberries
- ½ cup raspberries
- ½ cup blackberries
- 2 bananas, sliced, frozen
- 1 cup brewed green tea
- 2 teaspoon lemon juice

- 1 cup Greek yogurt

Directions:

- Follow the directions on the package and brew the green tea. Chill for 50 – 60 minutes.
- Pour green tea into a blender. Add all the berries, banana and yogurt and blitz until smooth.
- Stir in lemon juice.
- Pour into 3 – 4 glasses and serve.

Matcha Green Tea and Pineapple Smoothie

Preparation time: 5 minutes

Cooking time: 0 minutes

Number of servings: 2

Ingredients:

- 2 bananas, sliced
- 2 cups chopped kale
- 2 cups chopped pineapple
- 1 teaspoon matcha green tea powder
- Lemon juice to taste
- 1 cup soy milk
- Ice cubes, as required

Directions:

- Add banana, kale, pineapple, soymilk and ice cubes into a blender and blitz until smooth.
- Stir in lemon juice and matcha green tea powder just before serving. If you are using fresh pineapple, consume it right away. Keeping it for later will make it bitter.
- Pour into 2 glasses and serve.

Orange and Mango Green Tea Smoothie

Preparation time: 10 minutes

Cooking time: 0 minutes

Number of servings: 1

Ingredients:

- ½ cup fresh orange juice
- 1 small banana, sliced, frozen
- ½ cup frozen mango chunks
- 1 tablespoon Matcha green tea powder

Directions:

1. Add orange juice, banana, mango and green tea powder into a blender and blitz until smooth.
2. Pour into a glass and serve.

Parsley, Pineapple, and Banana Smoothie

Preparation time: 10 minutes

Cooking time: 0 minutes

Number of servings: 2

Ingredients:

- 2 bananas, sliced
- 1 cup packed parsley
- 2 cups chopped pineapple
- o teaspoons flaxseed meal or chia seeds (optional)
- ¼ cup chopped walnuts
- Ice cubes, as required

Directions:

1. Add bananas, parsley, pineapple, flaxseed meal or chia seeds if using, walnuts and ice cubes into a blender.

2. Blitz for 30 – 40 seconds or until smooth. If you are using fresh pineapple, consume it right away. Keeping it for later will make it bitter.

3. Pour into 2 glasses and serve.

Coconut Oil Latte

Preparation time: 3 minutes

Cooking time: 0 minutes

Number of servings: 2

Ingredients:

- 4 tablespoons vanilla soy milk or any other milk of your choice
- Stevia to taste
- 4 tablespoons coconut oil
- 2 cups brewed coffee

Directions:

1. Add coffee, coconut oil, milk and stevia into a blender.

2. Blend until well combined and frothy. It can take a couple of minutes. You can also make it in a frother.

3. Pour into mugs and serve.

Matcha Latte

Preparation time: 2 minutes

Cooking time: 2 minutes

Number of servings: 2

Ingredients:

- 1 – 2 teaspoons Matcha green tea powder
- ½ teaspoon chaga powder (optional)
- 2 tablespoons organic virgin coconut oil
- 1 cup hot filtered water
- 1 cup coconut milk, cold or heated
- ½ teaspoon turmeric powder

Directions:

1. Add Matcha powder, turmeric powder and chaga powder if using, into a small bowl. Add a little hot water and stir into a smooth paste.

2. Add coconut oil and stir until it is well combined.

3. Pour into a blender or frother. Add coconut milk and blend until creamy.

4. Pour into mugs and serve.

Golden Turmeric Latte

Preparation time: 3 minutes

Cooking time: 3 minutes

Number of servings: 1

Ingredients:

- 1 ½ cups coconut milk
- ½ teaspoon ground cinnamon
- A pinch black pepper
- A pinch cayenne pepper
- ½ teaspoon turmeric powder
- ½ teaspoon raw honey
- 2 slices fresh, peeled ginger

Directions:

1. Blend milk, honey, ginger and all the spices in a blender until smooth.

2. Transfer into a saucepan. Place the saucepan over medium flame and heat for about 3 minutes, until hot, making sure not to boil it.

3. Pour into a mug and serve.

Coconut Oil Hot Chocolate

Preparation time: 3 minutes

Cooking time: 5 minutes

Number of servings: 2

Ingredients:

1 cup full-fat coconut milk
1 cup filtered water
4 tablespoons grass-fed butter, unsalted
4 tablespoons raw cacao powder or cocoa powder
½ teaspoon ground cinnamon or to taste
2 tablespoons coconut oil
½ teaspoon vanilla extract

Directions:

1. Add water and coconut milk into a saucepan. Place the saucepan over medium flame.
2. When the mixture comes to a boil, turn off the heat.
3. Transfer the mixture into a blender or frother. Add butter, cocoa, cinnamon, oil and vanilla and blend until smooth and frothy.
4. Pour into mugs and serve.

Peach Green Iced Tea

Preparation time: 5 minutes

Cooking time: 15 minutes

Number of servings: 2

Ingredients:

- 1 tablespoon loose leaf green tea
- 1 ½ fresh peaches, pitted, sliced + extra to serve
- ½ cup apple juice
- 3 cups water

Directions:

1. Pour ½ cup of water and apple juice into a saucepan. Add peach slices and place the saucepan over medium flame.
2. When it begins to boil, lower heat and simmer for 10 - 12 minutes. Stir occasionally. Crush the peach as it cooks. Remove from heat and set aside to cool.
3. Pour the mixture through a fine wire mesh strainer placed over a bowl and discard the solids.
4. Pour remaining water into a pan and boil the water. Turn off the heat.
5. Place green tea leaves in an infuser, steep the green tea in it.
6. Combine green tea and peach mixture in a pitcher and place in the refrigerator for a couple of hours until very chill.
7. Fill glasses with crushed ice. Pour iced tea in it. Garnish with peach slices and serve.

Chapter 4: Breakfast

Green Goddess Scrambled Eggs

Preparation time: 10 minutes

Cooking time: 10 minutes

Number of servings: 2

Ingredients:

- ½ tablespoon extra-virgin olive oil
- Salt to taste
- 2 tablespoons thinly sliced fresh chives
- Freshly ground pepper to taste
- 1 tablespoon sour cream
- 3 cups packed baby kale
- 4 large eggs
- ½ tablespoon chopped fresh tarragon
- 1 tablespoon unsalted butter

Directions:

1. Place a skillet over medium-high flame. Add oil and let it heat. Once the oil is heated, add kale and a bit of salt and cook until it wilts.

2. Remove kale onto a plate.

3. Add eggs, salt and pepper into a bowl and whisk until frothy. Add chives and tarragon and stir well.

4. Add butter into the skillet. Once the butter melts, pour egg mixture and keep stirring until the eggs have begun to cook.

5. Add kale and mix well. Keep stirring until the eggs are soft cooked. Turn off the heat.

6. Add sour cream and mix gently.

7. Serve right away.

Mushroom Scrambled Eggs

Preparation time: 10 minutes

Cooking time: minutes

Number of servings: 4

Ingredients:

- 8 eggs
- 4 teaspoons mild curry powder
- 4 teaspoons extra-virgin olive oil
- 4 cups thinly sliced button mushrooms
- 4 teaspoons turmeric powder
- Mixture of seeds, to garnish
- 4 – 6 kale leaves, discard hard stems and ribs, chopped
- 2 bird's eye chili's, thinly sliced
- 2 teaspoons chopped parsley
- Salt to taste
- Rooster sauce to taste (optional)
- 2 – 3 tablespoons water

Directions:

1. To make spice paste: Combine water, turmeric powder, salt and curry powder in a bowl.

2. Place a pan over medium flame. Add oil. Once the oil is heated, add bird's eye chili and mushrooms and cook for a couple of minutes.

3. Add kale and cook until kale wilts.

4. Stir in the spice paste and eggs. Stir constantly and cook until eggs are soft cooked.

5. Stir in the parsley.

6. Serve hot.

Tofu Scramble with Kale and Sweet Potatoes

Preparation time: 10 minutes

Cooking time: 10 – 12 minutes

Number of servings: 4

Ingredients:

- 2 small sweet potatoes, scrubbed, chopped into ½ inch cubes
- 1 small red onion, chopped
- ½ teaspoon garlic powder
- 1 teaspoon salt
- 4 cups baby kale
- Salt to taste
- 2 tablespoons olive oil
- 2 packages (14 ounces each) extra-firm tofu, drained, crumbled
- 2 teaspoons ground cumin
- ½ teaspoon turmeric powder
- Pepper to taste

Directions:

1. Place a large skillet over medium-high flame. Add sweet potatoes and pour enough water to cover the sweet potatoes.

2. When it begins to boil, lower the heat to medium heat and cook for 3 minutes. Drain off the water from the skillet.

3. Add oil and onion into the skillet.

4. Increase the heat to medium-high heat. Cook for about 5 – 6 minutes.

5. Stir in the tofu, spices and salt. Heat thoroughly.
6. Stir in kale. Cook covered on low heat until kale wilts.
7. Serve hot.

Blueberry Banana Pancakes with Chunky Apple Compote

Preparation time: 10 minutes

Cooking time: 3 - 4 minutes per pancake

Number of servings: 3 - 4

Ingredients:

For pancakes:

- 3 bananas, sliced
- 2.6 ounces rolled oats
- 1/8 teaspoon salt
- 3 eggs
- 1 teaspoon baking powder
- 4.4 ounces blueberries
- Butter, to fry

For apple compote:

- 1 apple, peeled, cored, chopped into chunks
- ½ tablespoon lemon juice
- A tiny pinch salt
- 2 - 3 dates, pitted
- A large pinch ground cinnamon

Directions:

1. To make pancakes: Add oats into a dry blender and blend until you get fine powder.
2. Add baking powder, eggs, banana and salt and blitz until smooth.
3. Pour into a bowl. Add blueberries and fold gently. Cover and set aside for 10 minutes.

4. Place a nonstick pan over medium-high flame. Add a little butter and let it melt. Swirl the pan to spread the butter.

5. Pour about ¼ cup of the batter into the pan. Soon bubbles will be visible on top of the pancake.

6. Once the bottom side is golden brown, turn the pancake over and cook the other side. Remove the pancake onto a plate and serve with apple compote.

7. Repeat steps 4 – 6 and make the other pancakes similarly.

8. To make apple compote: Add apples, water, salt, dates, cinnamon and lemon juice and pulse until well combined and chunky.

Strawberry Chocolate Chip Buckwheat Pancakes

Preparation time: 5 minutes

Cooking time: 6 – 8 minutes per pancake

Number of servings: 8

Ingredients:

- 2 cups buckwheat flour
- 2 teaspoons baking powder
- ½ teaspoon kosher salt
- 4 tablespoons extra-virgin olive oil
- 2 large eggs
- ½ cup dairy-free dark chocolate chips
- 4 tablespoons coconut sugar
- 2 teaspoons ground cinnamon
- 1 ½ cups cashew milk or soy milk or almond milk, unsweetened
- 2 tablespoons vanilla extract
- 1 cup chopped strawberries

For optional toppings:

- Chopped strawberries
- Maple syrup
- Chocolate chips
- Ground flax seeds or hemp hearts or any other toppings of your choice

Directions:

1. Spray some olive oil cooking spray on a skillet and place it over medium flame.
2. Meanwhile, add flour, baking powder, salt, sugar and cinnamon into a bowl and stir until well combined.
3. Add eggs, vanilla oil and milk into another bowl and whisk until well combined.
4. Pour the egg mixture into the bowl of dry ingredients and mix until just incorporated, making sure not to over-mix.
5. Add chocolate chips and strawberries and fold gently.
6. Pour about ½ cup batter on the skillet and spread it out into a circle with a spatula, about 5 inches in diameter.
7. Soon bubbles will be visible on top of the pancake.
8. Once the bottom side is golden brown, turn the pancake over and cook the other side. Remove pancake onto a plate and keep warm.
9. Repeat steps 6 – 8 and make the other pancakes similarly.
10. Serve with optional toppings.

Apple Pancakes with Blackcurrant Compote

Preparation time: 10 minutes

Cooking time: 3 - 4 minutes per pancake

Number of servings: 8

Ingredients:

- 5.2 ounces porridge oats
- 2 teaspoons baking powder
- ¼ teaspoon salt
- 20 ounces semi-skimmed milk
- 4 teaspoons light olive oil
- 8.8 ounces plain flour
- 4 tablespoons caster sugar
- 4 apples, peeled, cored, cubed
- 4 egg whites

For blackcurrant compote:

- 8.4 ounces black currants, discard stalks
- 6 tablespoons water
- 4 tablespoons caster sugar

Directions:

1. To make blackcurrant compote: Mix together sugar, black currants and water in a skillet and place the skillet over medium flame.

2. Simmer on low heat, for about 10 minutes.

3. Combine oats, baking powder, salt, flour and caster sugar in a mixing bowl.

4. Add apple and stir. Add milk, about 1 ounce at a time and whisk well each time.

5. Once all the milk is added, whisk until smooth and free from lumps.

6. Beat the egg whites until stiff peaks are formed. Add egg whites into the batter and fold gently.

7. Place a nonstick pan over medium-high flame. Add a teaspoon of oil and let it heat. Swirl the pan to spread the oil.

8. Spoon about 1/8 of the batter into the pan. When the underside side is golden brown, turn the pancake over and cook the other side. Remove the pancake onto a plate and keep warm.

9. Repeat steps 7 – 8 and make the remaining pancakes similarly

10. Serve pancakes with black currant compote.

Chocolate Cream Pancake

Preparation time: 10 minutes

Cooking time: 4 – 5 minutes per pancake

Number of servings: 2

Ingredients:

For the pancakes:

- 2.1 ounces buckwheat flour
- 2 tablespoons ground flax seeds
- ½ teaspoon baking powder
- 2.1 ounces pea protein powder
- 2 – 4 tablespoons apple cider vinegar
- Stevia to taste
- 1 teaspoon olive oil + more if required
- 1 cup cannellini beans

For the chocolate cream:

- 2 tablespoons flax seed oil
- 2 tablespoons cocoa powder
- 2 tablespoons agave nectar

Directions:

1. Add buckwheat flour, pea protein, flax seeds, vinegar, baking powder, stevia, cannellini beans and ½ a cup of water into the food processor bowl. Process until smooth and well combined.
2. Pour the batter into a bowl. Let the batter rest for 5 minutes.
3. Place a nonstick pan over medium flame. Add oil. When the oil is heated pour about ½ the pancake mixture on the pan. Spread the batter if the batter is very thick. Soon bubbles will be visible on top.
4. When the underside is golden brown, turn the pancake over and cook the other side.
5. Repeat steps 3 - 4 and make the other pancake.
6. To make the chocolate cream: Mix together flax seed oil, cocoa and agave nectar in a bowl.
7. Serve warm pancakes with the chocolate cream and fruits of your choice.

Shakshuka

Preparation time: 10 - 12 minutes

Cooking time: 25 minutes

Number of servings: 4

Ingredients:

- 2 teaspoons extra-virgin olive oil
- 2 cloves garlic, peeled, finely chopped
- 2 Bird's eye chili's, finely chopped
- 2 teaspoons turmeric powder
- Pepper to taste
- 2 cans (14.1 ounces each) chopped tomatoes
- 2 tablespoons chopped parsley
- 3 ounces (about 1 medium) red onion, finely chopped
- ½ stalk celery, finely chopped
- 2 teaspoons ground cumin

- 2 teaspoons paprika or to taste
- 2.5 ounces kale leaves, chopped
- 4 medium eggs
- Salt to taste

Directions:

1. Place a deep skillet over medium-low flame. Add oil and let it heat. Once the oil is heated, stir in garlic, onion, celery and all the spices.

2. Sauté for a couple of minutes. Stir in the tomatoes.

3. Lower the heat and cook covered for about 20 minutes. Stir occasionally.

4. Stir in the kale and cook for about 5 minutes. If the sauce is visibly dry, add some water.

5. Make 4 cavities in the mixture (big enough for an egg to fit in), at different spots. Break an egg into each cavity.

6. Lower the heat and cook covered until the whites are cooked and the yolks are slightly runny or the way you prefer it cooked.

7. Serve hot.

Date and Walnut Porridge

Preparation time: 10 minutes

Cooking time: 10 minutes

Number of servings: 4

Ingredients:

- 4 cups milk of your choice
- 5 ounces buckwheat flakes
- 7 ounces strawberries, hulled
- 4 medjool dates, pitted, chopped
- 4 teaspoons walnut butter or 8 walnut halves, chopped

Directions:

1. Add milk and dates into a saucepan. Place the saucepan over medium flame.
2. When it is slightly hot, add buckwheat flakes and stir.
3. Stir often until the porridge is thick, as per your liking.
4. Add walnut butter and stir.
5. Serve in bowls topped with strawberries.

Healthy Matcha Green Tea Overnight Oats

Preparation time: 5 minutes

Cooking time: 0 minutes

Number of servings: 2

Ingredients:

- 1 cup old fashioned rolled oats
- Stevia to taste
- 1 teaspoon vanilla extract
- 1 teaspoon matcha green tea powder
- 1 1/3 cups unsweetened vanilla almond milk + extra to serve
- 20 drops almond extract

Directions:

1. Combine oats, stevia and matcha powder in a bowl.
2. Add almond milk, almond extract and vanilla extract and stir well.
3. Keep the bowl covered with plastic wrap and chill overnight.
4. Stir and serve in bowls with more milk and toppings of your choice if desired.

Choco- Chip Granola

Preparation time: 5 - 8 minutes

Cooking time: 20 minutes

Number of servings: 4

Ingredients:

- 3.5 ounces jumbo oats
- 1 ½ tablespoons light olive oil
- ½ tablespoon dark brown sugar
- 2 - 3 tablespoons chopped pecans
- 2 teaspoons butter
- 1 tablespoon rice malt syrup
- 1 ounce dark chocolate chips

Directions:

1. Prepare a baking sheet by lining it with parchment paper.
2. Place oats and pecans in a bowl and toss well.
3. Add oil, brown sugar, butter and malt syrup into a nonstick pan. Place the pan over medium-low heat and stir frequently until the mixture is warm, melts and is well combined. Turn off the heat before the mixture boils.
4. Transfer the mixture into the bowl of oats and mix until well combined.
5. Spread the mixture on a baking sheet lined with parchment paper.
6. Bake in an oven preheated to 320° F until golden brown around the edges, about 20 minutes.
7. When baked, take out the baking sheet and cool completely on your countertop.
8. Break into pieces. Add chocolate chips and mix well. Transfer into an airtight container. This can last for 2 weeks at room temperature.
9. Serve.

Smoked Salmon Omelet

Preparation time: 10 minutes

Cooking time: 5 minutes

Number of servings: 2

Ingredients:
- 4 medium eggs
- 1 teaspoon capers
- 2 teaspoons chopped parsley
- 7 ounces smoked salmon, sliced
- A handful rocket, chopped
- 2 teaspoons extra-virgin olive oil
- Salt and pepper to taste

Directions:
1. Whisk eggs in a bowl until nice and frothy.
2. Stir in capers, salmon, salt, pepper, parsley and rocket.
3. Place a nonstick pan over medium flame. Add a of teaspoon of oil. Once oil is heated, pour half the egg mixture. Swirl the pan to spread the egg mixture.
4. Cook on low heat until the omelet sets.
5. Remove omelet onto a plate and serve.
6. Repeat steps 3 – 5 and make the other omelet.

-

Buckwheat Superfood Muesli

Preparation time: 10 minutes

Cooking time: 0 minutes

Number of servings: 2

Ingredients:
- 1.4 ounces buckwheat flakes
- 1 ounce coconut flakes or desiccated coconut

- 1 ounce walnuts, chopped
- 7 ounces strawberries, chopped
- 0.7 ounce buckwheat puffs
- 8 medjool dates, pitted, chopped
- 0.7 ounce cocoa nibs
- 7 ounces plain Greek yogurt

Directions:

1. Add coconut flakes, walnuts, strawberries, dates, cocoa nibs, yogurt, buckwheat flakes and buckwheat puffs into a bowl and stir.
2. Divide into 2 bowls and serve.

Grain Bowl

Preparation time: 10 minutes

Cooking time: 5 minutes

Number of servings: 4

Ingredients:

- 2 tablespoons extra-virgin olive oil + extra to drizzle
- 2 bunches kale, discard hard stems and ribs, chopped
- 4 cups leftover cooked buckwheat or quinoa or brown rice or any other favorite grains of your choice
- 2 tomatoes, chopped
- 2 cloves garlic, peeled, finely chopped
- Pepper to taste
- 1 avocado, peeled, pitted, cubed
- Salt to taste

Directions:

1. Place a large nonstick pan over medium flame. Add oil. When the oil is heated, add garlic and stir constantly until golden brown.
2. Stir in the kale, salt and pepper and cook until it wilts.
3. Take 4 bowls and add a cup of cooked grains into each.

4. Divide the kale mixture, avocado and tomatoes equally among the bowls and serve.

Buckwheat and Eggs

Preparation time: 5 minutes

Cooking time: 10 minutes

Number of servings: 2

Ingredients:

- ½ cup buckwheat groats
- 4 tablespoons extra- virgin olive oil
- ½ cup fresh parsley, finely chopped
- Salt to taste
- 4 eggs
- 4 spring onions, finely chopped
- 2 tablespoons plain yogurt
- Pepper to taste

Directions:

1. Follow the directions on the package and cook the buckwheat groats.

2. Place a pan over medium heat. Add oil. When the oil is heated, add spring onions and sauté for a minute.

3. Add buckwheat, eggs and parsley and sauté until the eggs are cooked as per your preference

4. Add salt and pepper to taste and stir.

5. Divide into 2 bowls. Drizzle a tablespoon of yogurt on each and serve.

Savory Tempeh Breakfast Sandwich

Preparation time: 10 minutes

Cooking time: 10 – 12 minutes

Number of servings: 1

Ingredients:

- 1 ½ tablespoons soy sauce or tamari
- ½ tablespoon apple cider vinegar
- ½ teaspoon smoked paprika
- ½ package (from an 8 ounces package) tempeh, cut into thin slices
- 1 English muffin, split
- A handful baby spinach
- Dijon mustard to taste
- ¾ tablespoon maple syrup
- 2 small cloves garlic, minced
- Pepper to taste
- ½ tablespoon olive oil
- ¼ avocado, peeled, pitted, sliced
- Salt to taste

Directions:

1. Combine vinegar, maple syrup, soy sauce, garlic, pepper and paprika in a small bowl.
2. Place a skillet over medium flame. Add oil. When the oil is heated, place tempeh in the pan, without overlapping and cook until the underside is brown. Turn the sides of the tempeh slices and cook the other side until brown.
3. Add the sauce mixture and stir until well coated. Cook until dry. Flip the tempeh a couple of times while cooking.
4. Toast the muffin slices to the desired crispiness.
5. Spread a little ketchup and Dijon mustard over the cut part of the English muffin.
6. Place tempeh slices on the bottom half of the muffin. Layer with avocado slices and baby spinach.
7. Cover with the top half of the English muffin and serve.

Chapter 5: Soups

Greens and Grains Soup

Preparation time: 20 minutes

Cooking time: 45 minutes

Number of servings: 2 - 3

Ingredients:

- ½ cup whole grains of your choice like wheat berries, brown rice, barley etc., rinsed well
- 5 ounces kale, chopped (leaves and stems, but keep them separate)
- 1 clove garlic, peeled, minced
- Freshly ground pepper to taste
- ½ tablespoon extra-virgin olive oil + extra to drizzle
- 3 cups vegetable broth or chicken broth
- Salt to taste

Directions:

1. Place grains in a saucepan. Pour enough water to cover the grains. Place the saucepan over medium flame.

2. As it begins to boil, lower the heat and cook covered, until grains are cooked.

3. Drain in a colander.

4. Place a soup pot over medium-high flame. Add oil and let it heat.

5. Once the oil is heated, stir in the stalks of kale and sauté until tender.

6. Stir in garlic and cook for a few seconds until fragrant.

7. Pour stock and scrape the bottom of the pot to deglaze. Add grains. When the soup comes to a boil, add kale leaves and cook until kale wilts. Add salt and pepper to taste.

8. Ladle into soup bowls. Serve drizzled with some olive oil on top.

Winter Vegetable Soup with Butternut Squash & Cauliflower

Preparation time: 20 minutes

Cooking time: 20 - 25 minutes

Number of servings: 8

Ingredients:

- teaspoons olive oil
- cloves garlic, minced
- 2 stalks celery, thinly sliced
- 2 medium onions, chopped
- 1 pound cauliflower, cut into florets
- 1 ½ pounds butternut squash, peeled, deseeded, cubed
- 2 medium carrots, cut into thin half moons
- 1 teaspoon dried thyme
- ½ teaspoon chili flakes
- Salt to taste
- 2 tablespoons tomato paste
- 3 ½ cups vegetable broth
- 4 bay leaves
- 3 ½ cups water

- Pepper to taste
- ½ cup chopped fresh parsley

Directions:

1. Place a soup pot over medium flame.
2. Add oil. When the oil is heated, add onions and sauté until pink.
3. Stir in carrots, celery, garlic, chili flakes, salt and thyme. Sauté until the vegetables are slightly soft.
4. Add tomato paste and cook for a minute, stirring constantly.
5. Add squash, bay leaves, cauliflower and broth. Let it come to a boil.
6. Lower the heat and cover the pot partially with a lid. Cook until the vegetables are tender.
7. Remove the pot from heat and cool for about 10 minutes. Add about 4 cups of soup into a blender. Blend until smooth.
8. Pour the blended soup into the pot. Heat if desired.
9. Add parsley and stir.
10. Ladle into soup bowls and serve.

Beans and Farro Soup

Preparation time: 20 minutes

Cooking time: 45 minutes

Number of servings: 4

Ingredients:

- ½ cup farro, rinsed well
- 1 red onion, chopped
- 5 ounces kale, chopped (leaves and stems, but keep them separate)
- 5 ounces Swiss chard, chopped (leaves and stems, but keep them separate)
- 1 clove garlic, peeled, minced
- 1 inch fresh ginger, peeled, minced

- Freshly ground pepper to taste
- ½ tablespoon extra-virgin olive oil + extra to drizzle
- 4 cups vegetable broth
- Salt to taste
- 1 teaspoon Italian seasoning
- ½ cup chopped parsley
- 1 can (15 ounces) white beans, drained, rinsed

Directions:

1. Place farro in a saucepan. Pour enough water to cover the farro. Place the saucepan over medium flame.
2. As it begins to boil, lower the heat and cook covered, until farro turns tender.
3. Drain in a colander.
4. Place a soup pot over medium-high flame. Add oil and let it heat.
5. Once the oil is heated, add onion and cook until translucent. Stir in the stalks of Swiss chard and kale and sauté until tender.
6. Stir in ginger and garlic and cook for a few seconds until fragrant.
7. Pour stock and scrape the bottom of the pot to deglaze. Add cooked farro and beans. When the soup comes to a boil, add Swiss chard and kale leaves and cook until the greens wilt. Add Italian seasoning salt and pepper to taste.
8. Ladle into soup bowls. Serve drizzled with some olive oil on top.

Broccoli and Kale Green Soup

Preparation time: 15 minutes

Cooking time: 20 minutes

Number of servings: 4

Ingredients:

- 4 cups boiling water
- 2 tablespoons bouillon powder
- 4 cloves garlic, peeled, sliced
- 1 teaspoon ground coriander
- 1 pound courgette, sliced
- 1 bunch kale, chopped, discard hard stems and ribs
- 1 cup chopped parsley + few whole leaves to garnish
- 2 tablespoons olive oil
- 2 inches fresh ginger, peeled, sliced
- 2 inches fresh turmeric, peeled, grated or use 1 teaspoon turmeric powder
- 1 small head broccoli, cut into florets
- Juice of 2 limes
- Pepper to taste
- Zest of a lime, grated
- Himalayan pink salt to taste

Directions:

1. To make stock: Combine boiling hot water and stock in a saucepan. Set aside.
2. Place a soup pot over medium flame. Add oil. Once the oil is heated, add ginger and garlic and stir-fry for 30 - 40 seconds. Add turmeric powder, salt and coriander and stir for another 8 - 10 seconds.
3. Add a little water and mix well. Stir in the courgettes and stir until the slices are well coated with the spice mixture. Cook for about 2 - 3 minutes.
4. Pour stock and cook for a couple of minutes.
5. Stir in broccoli, lime juice and kale. Cook until kale and broccoli turns bright green and slightly tender. Remove the pot from heat and stir in parsley.
6. Transfer into a blender and blend until well pureed.

7. Ladle into soup bowls. Sprinkle lemon zest and parsley leaves on top and serve.

Miso Ramen Soup with Buckwheat Noodles

Preparation time: 20 - 25 minutes

Cooking time: 7 - 8 hours

Number of servings: 8

Ingredients:

For bone broth:

- 6.6 pounds beef bones or chicken carcasses or lamb bones
- 2 onions or leeks or carrots or celery, chopped into chunks
- 4 bay leaves
- 3 - 4 tablespoons apple cider vinegar
- 2 tablespoons black peppercorns

For noodles and vegetables:

- 24 ounces buckwheat noodles
- 8 heads Bok Choy, trimmed, thinly sliced
- 2 carrots, cut into matchsticks
- 4 inch piece fresh ginger root, peeled, grated
- 8 tablespoons lime juice
- 3 - 4 teaspoons tamari or soy sauce
- 2 tablespoons extra-virgin olive oil
- 14 ounces mixed mushrooms, sliced
- 1 small red cabbage, thinly sliced
- 12 spring onions, thinly sliced diagonally
- 4 tablespoons miso paste
- 1 cup chopped fresh cilantro

Directions:

1. To make stock: Add bones, onions, bay leaves, apple cider vinegar, and peppercorns into a large stock pot. Cover with enough water, such that the water level is about 3 inches above the bones.
2. Place the pot over high flame. When it comes to a boil, lower the heat and cook covered, for 6 hours if you are using chicken or about 12 hours if you are using beef bones or lamb bones.
3. Remove any scum that floats on top, time to time.
4. Place a strainer over a jar and strain the broth. The broth is ready to use.
5. To make noodles: Follow the directions on the package and cook the buckwheat noodles.
6. Drizzle oil over the strained and rinsed noodles. Toss well.
7. Pour 8 cups of broth into the stock pot. Store the remaining broth in the refrigerator and use it in some other recipe. If your broth is hot, proceed to the next step else heat up the broth.
8. Add ginger, lime juice, tamari, miso and spring onions into the stock pot and mix well.
9. Place equal quantities of Bok Choy, carrots, mushrooms and red cabbage into 8 soup bowls.
10. Pour a cup of broth into each cup. Divide the noodles among the bowls.
11. Garnish with cilantro and serve.

Strawberry Melon Soup with Mint

Preparation time: 15 minutes

Cooking time: 0 minutes

Number of servings: 4

Ingredients:

- 2 ½ cups ripe, peeled, seeded, cubed cantaloupe
- 2/3 cup fresh orange juice
- 1 ½ tablespoons fresh lime or lemon juice
- ½ cup ripe strawberries, hulled

- ¼ cup dry red wine
- 10 – 12 fresh mint leaves
- Stevia to taste (optional)

To serve:

- Sliced strawberries
- Mint leaves for

Directions:

1. Add cantaloupe and strawberries into a blender and blitz until smooth
2. Add orange juice, wine and lime juice and blend until smooth. Transfer into a bowl.
3. Add mint. Mix well. Add stevia if using. Mix well.
4. Cover the bowl with cling wrap and refrigerate for 3-4 hours.
5. Ladle into soup bowls. Garnish with sliced strawberries and mint leaves and serve.

Vegetarian Pasta Soup

Preparation time: 15 minutes

Cooking time: 20 minutes

Number of servings: 3

Ingredients:

- ½ tablespoon extra-virgin olive oil
- ¾ cup sliced white mushrooms
- 2 cloves garlic, peeled, minced
- 2 cups vegetable broth
- ½ can (from a 15 ounces can) tomato sauce
- ½ teaspoon kosher salt
- Crushed red pepper to taste
- Black pepper powder to taste
- ½ teaspoon dried basil
- 6 tablespoons grated parmesan cheese

- ¼ cup diced red onions
- 1 small zucchini, diced
- 2 tablespoons dry red wine
- ½ can (from a 14.5 ounces can) petite diced tomatoes
- ½ tablespoon Italian seasoning
- ¼ teaspoon garlic salt
- 1 cup buckwheat noodles
- A handful fresh parsley, chopped, to garnish

Directions:

1. Place a soup pot over medium high heat. Add oil. When the oil is heated, add onion, garlic and mushroom and sauté for 2-3 minutes.

2. Stir in the zucchini and sauté for a couple of minutes. Add wine and stir.

3. When the mixture begins to boil, add broth, tomato sauce, diced tomatoes, basil, salt and spices.

4. Once it starts boiling, lower heat to medium low and stir in the buckwheat noodles. Cook until the noodles are al dente. Remove from heat and add Parmesan cheese. Stir.

5. Ladle into soup bowls. Garnish with parsley and serve.

Caldo de Res (Mexican Beef Soup)

Preparation time: 20 minutes

Cooking time: 50 – 60 minutes

Number of servings: 4

Ingredients:

- 1 pound beef shank with bone
- 1 teaspoon salt or to taste
- ½ medium red onion, chopped + extra finely chopped, to garnish
- 1 bird's eye chili, sliced
- 2 cups water

- 1 ½ cups beef broth
- 1 medium carrot, peeled, coarsely chopped
- 1 small potato, quartered
- 1 chayote, peeled, chopped into chunks
- 1/8 cup sliced pickled jalapenos
- ½ cup chopped, fresh cilantro, divided
- 2 radishes, quartered + extra to serve
- ½ tablespoon olive oil
- 1 teaspoon black pepper or to taste
- ½ can (from a 14.5 ounce can) diced tomatoes
- 1 ear corn, husked, cut into thirds
- 1 small head cabbage, cored, cut into wedges
- Lime juice to taste

Directions:

1. Chop the meat from the beef bones (leave some meat on the bones as well) into ½ inch pieces.

2. Place a heavy soup pot or any other heavy pot like a Dutch oven over medium flame. Add oil and swirl the pot so the oil spreads all over the bottom of the pot.

3. Once oil is heated, add meat, bones, salt and pepper and mix well.

4. Once it turns brown, add chopped onions and cook until the onions are light brown, stirring frequently. Add tomatoes and broth. The broth should cover the bones and be at least ½ an inch above the bones. If the broth is not covering the bones, pour some water to keep it covered.

5. When it comes to a boil, lower the heat and cover the pot loosely with a lid. Simmer until the meat is tender.

6. Add the remaining water and continue simmering. Add carrots, bird's eye chili, half the cilantro, potatoes, chayote and corn. Cook until the potatoes and chayote are tender.

7. Add the cabbage and simmer for another 10 minutes. Turn off the heat.

8. Ladle into soup bowls. Garnish with jalapenos, finely chopped onions and the remaining cilantro over it.

9. Pour some lime juice into each bowl and top with radishes.

Cioppino

Preparation time: 10 minutes

Cooking time: 45 minutes

Number of servings: 3 – 4

Ingredients:

- 2 tablespoons extra-virgin olive oil
- 1 red onion, minced
- ½ fennel bulb, chopped, set aside the fronds
- 1 clove garlic, peeled, thinly sliced
- ¼ teaspoon red pepper flakes
- Freshly ground pepper to taste
- ½ teaspoon dried oregano
- Salt to taste
- ¾ cup dry red wine
- 4 ounces bottled clam juice
- ½ can (from a 28 ounces can) crushed tomatoes
- 1 cup water
- 1 strip orange zest (about an inch)
- 6 mussels, scrubbed
- ½ pound shrimp, peeled, deveined
- 6 littleneck clams, scrubbed
- ½ pound skinless halibut, cut into 1 inch pieces
- 1 bay leaf
- A handful fresh parsley, chopped, to serve

To serve:

- 3 – 4 lemon wedges
- Baguette slices

Directions:

1. Place a soup pot over medium flame. Add oil. When the oil is heated, add onion and fennel and cook until tender.

2. Stir in garlic, red pepper flakes, oregano, salt and pepper. Cook for a few seconds until you have a nice aroma.

3. Stir in wine and let it cook until it is half its original quantity. Deglaze the pot simultaneously.

4. Stir in tomatoes, water, orange zest, clam juice and bay leaf.

5. Cook on low for about 12 - 15 minutes, stir once in a while. Discard the bay leaf and orange zest strip.

6. Stir in the clams and simmer for 5 minutes, covering while cooking.

7. Now place mussels in a single layer followed by shrimp and finally halibut. You are not supposed to stir now.

8. Keep the pot covered and continue cooking for about 5 minutes or until most of the clams and mussels open up. Discard any unopened ones.

9. Add salt and pepper to taste and stir now.

10. Ladle into soup bowls. Garnish with fennel fronds and serve with toasted baguette slices and lemon wedges.

Bitter Greens with Cheese Dumplings Soup

Preparation time: 45 minutes

Cooking time: 20 minutes

Number of servings: 8

Ingredients:

- 2 cups lightly packed, freshly grated parmesan cheese
- 1 ½ cups fine dry breadcrumbs
- 8 large eggs, lightly beaten
- 4 tablespoons extra-virgin olive oil
- 16 cups low-sodium chicken stock or broth

- 2 cups lightly packed, freshly grated Pecorino Romano cheese + extra to serve
- A handful fresh flat-leaf parsley, finely chopped
- 4 cloves garlic, peeled, minced
- Freshly ground pepper to taste
- 1 pound red chicory, coarsely chopped
- Salt to taste

Directions:

1. Prepare a baking sheet by lining it with cling wrap.
2. Add parmesan and pecorino cheese into a bowl and mix well.
3. Add eggs, breadcrumbs, parsley and 2 cloves of minced garlic and mix until you get soft dough.
4. Make small balls of the mixture (about ¾ inch diameter) and place on the baking sheet. You may need to moisten your hands with some water to make the balls.
5. Place the baking sheet in the refrigerator for 30 minutes.
6. Place a soup pot over medium flame. Add oil and let it heat. When the oil is heated, add 2 cloves minced garlic and cook for a few seconds until aromatic.
7. Stir in the chicory and cook until slightly brown.
8. Pour stock and bring to a boil.
9. Lower the heat and add the dumplings into the pot. Simmer for a few minutes until the dumplings will be floating.
10. Add salt and pepper to taste.
11. Ladle into soup bowls. Garnish with pecorino and serve.

Lovage, Lettuce, Pea and Cucumber Soup

Preparation time: 10 minutes

Cooking time: 30 minutes

Number of servings: 6- 8

Ingredients:

- 3 tablespoons butter
- 2 teaspoons fresh thyme leaves, chopped
- 4 little gem lettuces, finely shredded
- 1 cucumber, diced
- 2 red onions, finely chopped
- Freshly ground pepper to taste
- 6 – 7 cups vegetable stock
- 1 cup peas
- 2 small handfuls lovage leaves, chopped (keep the leaves and stalks separate)

To serve:

- Thick yogurt
- 4 – 5 tablespoons crème fraiche

Directions:

1. Place a large saucepan over medium-low flame. Add butter and wait for it to melt.
2. Once butter melts, add onion, salt and thyme and cook until onion turns pink.
3. Stir in lovage stalks. Add stock after about 2 minutes and cook for about 12 minutes.
4. Add cucumber, lettuces, peas and most of the lovage leaves. Cook for about 5 minutes.
5. Ladle into soup bowls. Spoon some crème fraiche and yogurt on top. Top with retained lovage leaves and serve.

Chapter 6: Lunch Recipes

Salmon Super Salad

Preparation time: 10 minutes

Cooking time: 0 minutes

Number of servings: 2

Ingredients:

- 3.5 ounces rocket
- 7 ounces smoked salmon slices
- 3.5 ounces chicory leaves
- 1 medium avocado, peeled, pitted, sliced
- 2 tablespoons capers
- 2 tablespoons extra-virgin olive oil
- A handful fresh parsley, chopped
- A handful walnuts, chopped
- 2 large medjool dates, pitted, chopped
- Juice of ½ lemon
- A handful lovage leaves, chopped
- 1 medium red onion, chopped
- A handful celery leaves, chopped

Directions:

1. Add all the greens into a large bowl and toss well.
2. Add salmon, avocado, capers, walnuts, dates and red onions into another bowl and toss well.
3. Add lemon juice and oil and toss well.
4. Spread salmon mixture over the greens and serve.

Green Juice Salad

Preparation time: 10 minutes

Cooking time: 0 minutes

Number of servings: 2

Ingredients:

- 4 large handfuls kale leaves, torn
- A handful flat-leaf parsley
- A handful lovage leaves
- 2 large handfuls rocket
- 1 medium green apple, cored, sliced
- Salt to taste
- ½ cup chopped walnuts
- Pepper to taste
- 2 tablespoons extra-virgin olive oil
- Juice of a lemon
- 6 celery sticks with leaves, chopped
- 1 inch ginger, grated

Directions:

1. Add kale, parsley, lovage, rocket, apple, ginger and celery into a bowl and toss well.
2. Add salt, pepper, lemon juice and olive oil and toss well.
3. Garnish with walnuts and serve.

Broccoli, Edamame & Cabbage Millet Salad

Preparation time: 10 minutes

Cooking time: 30 minutes

Number of servings: 3

Ingredients:

- 3 tablespoons extra-virgin olive oil
- 1 small red onion, minced
- Pepper to taste
- 1 cup cooked, shelled edamame
- 3 tablespoons white wine vinegar
- ½ cup millets
- 1 cup water
- Salt to taste
- ¾ cup chopped red cabbage
- ¾ cup chopped broccoli florets
- 2 tablespoons chopped, dried apricots

Directions:

1. Add millets and water into a saucepan. Place the saucepan over medium flame.

2. When it begins to boil, lower the heat and cook covered, until dry. Turn off the heat and let it sit for 10 minutes. Uncover and fluff with a fork. Let it cool for a few minutes.

3. Add millets, onion, cabbage, broccoli, edamame, oil, vinegar, salt and pepper into a bowl and toss well.

4. Set aside for a while for the flavors to blend in.

5. Toss well.

6. Scatter apricots on top and serve.

Salmon Pasta Salad with Lemon & Capers

Preparation time: 10 minutes

Cooking time: 20 minutes

Number of servings: 4

Ingredients:

- 6 ounces whole-wheat penne pasta
- 2 large red bell peppers, chopped
- Zest of ½ lemon, grated
- Juice of 2 lemons
- 2 shallots, minced
- 12 kalamata olives, pitted, sliced
- 4 handfuls rocket
- 4 frozen, skinless, wild salmon fillets
- 4 cloves garlic, peeled, grated
- 4 tablespoons capers
- 2 teaspoons extra-virgin olive oil
- 2 tablespoons rapeseed oil or any other oil of your choice

Directions:

1. Follow the directions on the package and cook the pasta.

2. Place a pan over medium flame. Add rapeseed oil. Once the oil is heated, add red bell pepper and cook covered for 4 - 5 minutes or until slightly tender.

3. Move the red peppers from the pan to a plate and add salmon into the pan. Cook covered for 7 - 8 minutes or until the salmon flakes easily when pierced with a fork.

4. Meanwhile, add lemon juice, lemon zest, garlic, capers, shallot and olives into a large bowl and mix well.

5. Add pasta, salmon and red pepper and toss well. Sprinkle pepper on top. Drizzle oil. Toss well.

6. Cover and set aside until use.

7. Add rocket just before serving. Toss well and serve.

California Kale Cobb Salad

Preparation time: 10 minutes

Cooking time: 20 minutes

Number of servings: 2

Ingredients:

For the salad:

- 2 slices turkey bacon
- ½ avocado, peeled, pitted, diced
- ½ can (from a 15 ounces can) water packed artichoke heart quarters, drained
- 1 bunch kale, discard hard stem and ribs, leaves thinly sliced
- ½ cup halved grape or cherry tomatoes
- 8 ounces cooked chicken, diced
- ½ cup sliced strawberries
- 2 hardboiled eggs, peeled, quartered lengthwise
- ½ cup crumbled goat cheese

For the dressing:

- ¼ cup olive oil mayonnaise
- 1 finely chopped tablespoon Italian parsley
- 1 small clove garlic, peeled, minced
- Pepper to taste
- 1 tablespoon fresh lemon juice
- ½ tablespoon Dijon mustard
- Salt to taste (optional)
- 2 scallions, thinly sliced, to garnish

Directions:

1. Prepare a baking sheet by lining it with foul. Lay the bacon strips on the baking sheet.
2. Bake the bacon in an oven preheated to 350° F until brown and crisp, about 18 - 20 minutes, flipping sides halfway through baking.
3. When cool enough to handle, chop into small pieces and set aside.
4. To make the dressing: Add mayonnaise, parsley, garlic, pepper, lemon juice, mustard and salt into a bowl. Whisk well. Cover and set aside for a while for the flavors to set in.
5. Divide the kale leaves onto 2 serving plates.
6. Layer with equal quantities of avocado, artichoke hearts, tomatoes, bacon, strawberries and chicken in any manner you desire.
7. Sprinkle scallions on top. Place 4 slices of egg on the salad. Scatter goat cheese on top.
8. Divide the dressing into 2 small bowls. Serve the dressing on the side.

Fresh Fruit and Kale Salad

Preparation time: 15 minutes

Cooking time: 0 minutes

Number of servings: 8

Ingredients:

For the salad:

- 8 - 10 cups kale, discard hard ribs and stems, chopped
- 1 cup blackberries
- 1 cup blueberries
- 1 cup raspberries
- 2 cups sliced strawberries
- 1 cup cubed ripe mango
- 2 pears, peeled, deseeded, chopped into small cubes

- ½ cup chopped walnuts, toasted if desired

For the dressing:

- 6 tablespoons apple cider vinegar
- 4 tablespoons raw honey (optional)
- Freshly ground pepper to taste
- 6 tablespoons extra- virgin olive oil
- 4 tablespoons Dijon mustard
- Sea salt to taste

Directions:

1. Add apple cider vinegar, honey, oil, mustard, salt and pepper into a small bowl and whisk until well combined.

2. Add all the berries, mango, pears and kale into a bowl and toss well.

3. Pour dressing over it. Toss well and serve garnished with walnuts.

Warm Chicory Salad with Mushrooms

Preparation time: 10 minutes

Cooking time: 8 – 10 minutes

Number of servings: 2 – 3

Ingredients:

- 1 tablespoon minced shallot
- Salt to taste
- ¼ cup extra-virgin olive oil
- 2 ounces oyster mushrooms, sliced
- ½ Belgian endive, cut into 1 inch pieces
- ½ small head escarole, use the inner pale colored leaves only, chopped into 1 inch pieces
- ¼ cup shaved Parmesan cheese
- 1 tablespoon sherry vinegar
- Freshly ground pepper to taste

- 2 ounces shiitake mushrooms, cut into thick slices
- 1 sprig thyme
- ½ small head radicchio
- 2 tablespoons chopped flat-leaf parsley

Directions:

1. To make dressing: Add vinegar, salt and pepper into a bowl and whisk well. Let it rest for 10 minutes.
2. Add 3 tablespoons oil and whisk well. Cover and set aside.
3. Place a skillet over medium flame. Add a tablespoon of oil. When the oil is heated, add mushrooms, salt, pepper and thyme cook until brown. Stir occasionally.
4. Transfer the mushrooms into a bowl. Throw off the thyme.
5. Pour dressing over the mushrooms and toss well.
6. Add endive, escarole, radicchio and parsley and toss well. Taste and add more salt and pepper if required.
7. Scatter cheese and toss well.
8. Serve.

Courgette and Lovage Pasta

Preparation time: 10 minutes

Cooking time: 20 minutes

Number of servings: 2

Ingredients:

- 2 courgettes, trimmed, sliced into ribbons using a peeler
- 1 ½ tablespoons olive oil
- 1 clove garlic, finely chopped
- ¼ cup lovage leaves, finely shredded
- 3 ounces ricotta, chopped into chunks
- 7 ounces dried, whole-wheat penne or fusilli
- Salt to taste
- ¼ teaspoon grated lemon zest
- Freshly ground pepper to taste

- 3 ounces parmesan cheese, grated + extra to serve

Directions:

1. Follow the directions on the package and cook the pasta. Retain a little of the cooked water and drain off the rest.
2. Meanwhile, place a pan over medium-high flame. Add oil and wait for it to heat.
3. Once oil is heated, add courgettes, salt and pepper and cook until light golden.
4. Stir in lemon zest and garlic and cook for a few seconds until you get a nice aroma.
5. Add pasta, parmesan, ricotta and a little of the retained pasta cooked water. Toss well.
6. Divide into bowls. Garnish with parmesan and serve.

Strawberry Buckwheat Tabbouleh

Preparation time: 10 minutes

Cooking time: 15 – 20 minutes

Number of servings: 2

Ingredients:

- 2/3 cup buckwheat
- 1 avocado, peeled, pitted, cut into small cubes
- 1 medium red onion, chopped
- 2 tablespoons capers
- 1 1/3 cups strawberry slices
- Juice of a lemon
- 2 tablespoons ground turmeric
- 2 small tomatoes, diced
- ¼ cup pitted medjool dates
- 1 ½ cups parsley
- 2 tablespoons extra-virgin olive oil
- 2 handfuls arugula

Directions:

1. Follow the directions on the package and cook buckwheat, adding turmeric while cooking.
2. Once cooked, drain in a colander.
3. After the buckwheat cools, add into a bowl. Add avocado, onion, capers, tomatoes, dates and parsley and toss well.
4. Add strawberries, lemon juice and oil and toss well.
5. Spread a handful of arugula on each of 2 plates.
6. Divide the salad among the plates and place over the arugula.

Spring Vegetable & Cauliflower Tabbouleh

Preparation time: 15 minutes

Cooking time: 15 minutes

Number of servings: 2

Ingredients:

- 1 pound cauliflower, grated with the large holes of the grater
- 2 ½ tablespoons hot vegetable stock
- ½ courgette, cubed
- 1 teaspoon golden caster sugar
- 1 ½ tablespoons extra-virgin olive oil + extra to serve
- 1 tablespoon olive oil
- A handful fresh mint leaves, finely chopped
- 1 tablespoon olive oil
- 2.5 ounces fine asparagus, cut into small pieces, leaving the tips whole
- Zest of 1 lemon, grated
- Juice of ½ lemon
- 1 tablespoon capers, drained, chopped
- Salt to taste
- A large handful parsley leaves
- ½ bunch spring onions, sliced
- Pepper to taste

Directions:

1. Place a skillet over medium flame. Add ½ tablespoon olive oil. When the oil is heated, add cauliflower, salt and pepper to taste and cook covered for about 3 minutes. Stir every minute.

2. Add stock and mix well. Continue cooking for another 2 - 3 minutes or until dry. Turn off the heat and transfer onto a plate. Let it cool.

3. Place a pan over high flame. Add ½ tablespoon olive oil. When the oil is heated, add asparagus pieces, salt, pepper and courgette and cook until it is golden. Stir often.

4. Stir in the asparagus tips and cook for a couple of minutes. Turn off the heat and let the vegetables cool.

5. Meanwhile, add sugar, extra-virgin olive oil, sugar, capers, salt, pepper, lemon juice and zest into another bowl and whisk well. Let the dressing meld while the vegetables are cooling.

6. Once cooled, add cooked vegetables, cauliflower and spring onions into a large bowl and toss well.

7. Pour dressing on the salad. Toss well. Trickle more oil on top and serve.

Buckwheat Crepes

Preparation time: 15 minutes

Cooking time: 20 minutes

Number of servings: 8

Ingredients:

- ½ cup raw buckwheat groats or ½ cup buckwheat flour
- 2/3 cup unsweetened almond milk
- 1 teaspoon vanilla extract
- ¼ teaspoon salt
- 3 eggs
- 1 tablespoon maple syrup (optional)
- ½ teaspoon ground cinnamon (optional)

Directions:

1. If you are using buckwheat groats, add them into a blender and blend until you get fine powder.
2. Add milk, vanilla, salt, eggs, maple syrup and cinnamon and blend until smooth. Pour into a bowl.
3. Place a crepe pan or nonstick pan over medium-high flame. Spray some cooking spray over the pan. Let the pan heat.
4. Spoon about ¼ cup of the batter into the pan. Simultaneously swirl the pan to spread the batter.
5. When the crepe is set, turn the crepe over and cook the other side for about ½ a minute. Remove onto a plate.
6. Repeat steps 3 – 5 and make the remaining crepes.
7. Place fillings of your choice and serve the crepes.

Buckwheat Stir Fry with Kale, Peppers & Artichokes

Preparation time: 10 minutes

Cooking time: 15 minutes

Number of servings: 4

Ingredients:

For buckwheat:

- ¾ cup roasted buckwheat groats, uncooked, rinsed a few times
- ¼ teaspoon Himalayan pink salt
- 1 ½ cups water

For stir-fry:

- ½ bunch kale, discard hard stems and ribs, finely chopped
- 2 large bell peppers of any color, thinly sliced
- 2 tablespoons coconut oil, divided
- ¼ cup finely chopped basil
- ¼ cup finely chopped parsley
- 2 large cloves garlic, peeled, minced

- 1 cup marinated artichoke hearts, drained, chopped
- Salt to taste

Directions:

1. Add buckwheat, salt and water into a saucepan. Place the saucepan over medium flame.

2. Cover the saucepan with a lid and let it come to a boil.

3. Lower the heat and simmer for 10 - 12 minutes. Let it remain covered all the time.

4. Turn off the heat and let it rest for 3 minutes. Uncover and loosen the buckwheat grains using a fork.

5. Place a wok over medium flame. Add ½ tablespoon of oil. When the oil is heated, add garlic and cook for a few seconds until aromatic.

6. Stir in kale and a bit of salt and cook until it wilts. Remove the kale into a bowl.

7. Add ½ tablespoon oil into the wok. Stir in bell pepper and a bit of salt and cook until tender. Remove the bell peppers from the pan and place it along with kale.

8. Lower the heat to low heat. Add a tablespoon of oil. When the oil is heated, add buckwheat and stir such that buckwheat is coated in oil. Remove the pan from heat.

9. Stir in kale and bell peppers.

10. Also add artichokes, herbs and salt and toss well.

11. Serve.

Chicken and Kale Curry

Preparation time: 20 minutes

Cooking time: 60 minutes

Number of servings: 2

Ingredients:

- 7 ounces skinless, boneless chicken thighs
- ½ tablespoon olive oil
- A large handful kale, discard hard stems and ribs, torn

- 2 teaspoon finely chopped ginger
- 1 teaspoon turmeric powder
- 1 birds eye chili, finely chopped
- ½ tablespoon curry powder
- ½ can (from a 14 ounces can) chopped tomatoes
- 2 cups chicken stock
- ½ tablespoon olive oil
- 1 red onion, diced
- 1 tablespoon turmeric powder
- 2 cloves garlic, crushed
- ½ tablespoon chopped ginger
- 1 pod cardamom
- ½ cup light coconut milk
- Chopped cilantro, to garnish

Directions:

1. Sprinkle ½ tablespoon turmeric powder all over the chicken. Drizzle ½ teaspoon of oil over it and stir well. Cover and set aside for 30 minutes.

2. Place a nonstick pan over medium flame. Add chicken and cook until brown on the outside and well-cooked inside.

3. Transfer the chicken into a bowl.

4. Add the rest of the oil into the pan. Add onion, garlic, chili and ginger and cook until onion is pink.

5. Stir in remaining turmeric powder and curry powder. Stir for about a minute.

6. Stir in the stock, tomatoes, cardamom and coconut milk. Cook on low heat for about 20 minutes.

7. Add chicken and kale and cook for a few minutes, until kale wilts. Turn off the heat.

8. Serve over cooked buckwheat or any other cooked grain of your choice, garnished with cilantro.

Crispy Turmeric Roasted Potatoes

Preparation time: 10 minutes

Cooking time: 30 minutes

Number of servings: 3

Ingredients:

- ½ large red onion, chopped
- 3 medium potatoes, peeled, cut into bite size cubes
- Salt to taste
- 2 teaspoons curry powder (optional)
- 2 teaspoons turmeric powder
- Pepper to taste
- 2 tablespoons olive oil
- 2 cloves garlic, minced

Directions:

1. Place potatoes and onion in a bowl. Sprinkle garlic, salt, pepper, turmeric and curry powder over it and toss well.

2. Prepare a baking sheet by lining it with parchment paper.

3. Spread the potato mixture on the baking sheet, without overlapping.

4. Bake in an oven preheated to 320° F until golden brown around the edges and cooked through, about 30 minutes. Stir the potatoes occasionally.

5. When baked, take out the baking sheet and cool.

Buckwheat Pancakes

Preparation time: 25 minutes

Cooking time: 15 minutes

Number of servings: 3

Ingredients:

For dry ingredients:

- ½ cup buckwheat flour
- ½ cup 1:1 gluten-free baking flour
- 1 tablespoon honey or maple syrup
- ¼ teaspoon salt
- 1 teaspoon baking powder
- ¼ teaspoon ground cinnamon

For wet ingredients:

- ¾ cup almond milk or any other milk of your choice
- 2 tablespoons butter, melted + extra to make pancakes
- 2 eggs, separated
- ½ cup blueberries

Directions:

1. Add all the dry ingredients i.e. flours, honey, salt, baking powder and cinnamon into a mixing bowl and stir.

2. Whisk the whites with an electric hand mixer until stiff peaks are formed.

3. Add milk, butter and yolks into another bowl and whisk well.

4. Pour the milk mixture into the bowl of dry ingredients and stir until just combined, making sure not to over-mix.

5. Fold in the whites. Be gentle while folding.

6. Place a nonstick pan over medium-high flame. Add a little butter and let it melt. Swirl the pan to spread the butter.

7. Pour about ¼ cup of the batter into the pan. Scatter a few blueberries on top. Soon bubbles will be visible on top of the pancake.

8. Once the bottom side is golden brown, turn the pancake over and cook the other side. Remove pancake onto a plate and serve with apple compote.

9. Repeat steps 6 - 8 and make the other pancakes similarly.

Kale And Feta Frittata

Preparation time: 10 minutes

Cooking time: 30 minutes

Number of servings: 2 - 3

Ingredients:

- 4 eggs, beaten lightly
- 2 ounces feta cheese, crumbled
- 1 teaspoon dried dill
- ½ teaspoon butter
- 1 ½ cups fresh baby kale
- 1 tablespoon heavy cream
- Salt to taste

Directions:

1. Combine eggs, feta, dill, kale, cream and salt in a bowl.
2. Place a small ovenproof skillet over medium flame.
3. Add butter. When butter melts, pour the egg mixture into the skillet. Spread the kale evenly.
4. Cook for about 3 - 4 minutes, undisturbed. Turn off the heat.
5. Bake in an oven preheated to 350° F until eggs are set.
6. Cool for a few minutes. Cut into wedges and serve.

Parsley Detox Wrap

Preparation time: 10 minutes

Cooking time: 2 minutes

Number of servings: 4

Ingredients:

- 4 cups finely chopped fresh parsley
- 12 – 15 cherry tomatoes, quartered
- 1 cucumber, diced
- 2 teaspoons extra-virgin olive oil
- 2 ripe avocados, peeled, pitted, cubed
- Salt to taste
- 1 cup raw sunflower seeds
- Juice of 2 limes
- 4 whole wheat tortillas

Directions:

1. Add parsley, tomatoes, cucumber, oil, avocados, salt, sunflower seeds and lime juice into a bowl and toss well.
2. Warm the tortillas following the instructions on the package.
3. Divide the mixture among the tortillas. Roll the tortillas and place with its seam side down.
4. Serve.

Roast Beef Wrap

Preparation time: 10 minutes

Cooking time: 2 minutes

Number of servings: 4

Ingredients:

- 1 cup part-skim ricotta cheese
- 1 teaspoon grated lemon zest
- ½ teaspoon minced garlic

- 4 whole-wheat tortillas
- 12 ounces, lean, thinly sliced roast beef
- 2/3 - 1 cup chopped parsley
- 4 teaspoon fresh lemon juice
- Salt to taste
- 2 red bell peppers, thinly sliced

Directions:

1. Add parsley, ricotta, salt, garlic, lemon juice and zest into a bowl and toss well.
2. Warm the tortillas following the instructions on the package.
3. Divide the mixture among the tortillas. Wrap like a burrito.
4. Serve.

Chickpea, Quinoa and Turmeric Curry

Preparation time: 10 minutes

Cooking time: 45 minutes

Number of servings: 3

Ingredients:

- 8.8 ounces new potatoes, halved
- 1 ½ teaspoons ground turmeric
- ½ teaspoon chili flakes
- ½ teaspoon ground coriander
- ½ teaspoon ground ginger
- 1 cup coconut milk
- ½ can (from a 14.1 ounces can) chickpeas, drained, rinsed
- 2 cloves garlic, crushed
- ½ tablespoon tomato puree
- Salt to taste
- ½ can (from a 14.1 ounces can) chickpeas, drained, rinsed
- ½ bunch kale, discard hard stems and ribs, sliced
- Pepper to taste

- 3.2 ounces quinoa
- 5 ounces hot water

Directions:

1. Cook the potatoes in a saucepan of water until fork tender. Drain and place it in a pan.

2. Add coconut milk, tomato puree, tomatoes and all the spices along with salt and stir.

3. Place the pan over high heat. When it begins to boil, add quinoa and hot water.

4. Cook covered on low, until half the liquid in the pan has been absorbed. Stir often.

5. Stir in the chickpeas. Continue cooking covered, stirring often.

6. When nearly dry, add kale and stir. Continue cooking covered, until dry.

7. Turn off the heat and let it rest for 5 minutes. Fluff with a fork and serve.

Chapter 7: Snacks

Buckwheat Granola

Preparation time: 10 minutes

Cooking time: 20 - 25 minutes

Number of servings: 8 - 10

For granola:

- ¾ cup buckwheat groats
- ½ cup chopped walnuts or any other nuts of your choice
- ¾ cup gluten-free rolled oats
- ¼ cup unsweetened coconut flakes
- 1 ½ tablespoons coconut sugar or sweetener of your choice
- ½ teaspoon ground cinnamon
- ¼ cup maple syrup or more to taste
- 3 tablespoons dried blueberries or dark chocolate chips
- 1 tablespoon chia seeds
- ¼ teaspoon sea salt
- 2 tablespoons coconut oil or avocado oil or olive oil
- 1 ½ tablespoons nut butter or seed butter (optional)

Directions:

1. Combine buckwheat groats, coconut, coconut sugar, cinnamon, oats, chia seeds and salt in a bowl.
2. Heat oil and maple syrup over medium flame, until well combined and smooth.
3. Stir in nut butter if using. Turn off the heat and drizzle over the buckwheat mixture.
4. Stir until well combined.
5. Transfer the mixture on a baking sheet and spread it evenly.
6. Bake in an oven preheated to 325° F until nice and aromatic and golden brown, about 20 – 25 minutes. Stir after about 10 – 12 minutes of baking.
7. Cool for a few minutes. Add blueberries if using and stir. If you want to add chocolate, let it cool to room temperature before adding the chocolate.
8. Once cooled, transfer into an airtight container. It can last for about 2 weeks.
9. Serving it with fruits and milk will make it a filling breakfast.

Chocolate Coconut Vegan Energy Balls

Preparation time: 20 minutes

Cooking time: 0 minutes

Number of servings: 10

Ingredients:

- 1/3 cup almonds
- 1 tablespoon ground flax seeds
- 2/3 cup old fashioned oats
- 2 tablespoons unrefined coconut oil, melted
- ¼ cup unsweetened cocoa powder
- 1/8 teaspoon fine sea salt
- 8 ounces medjool dates, pitted, soaked in water if they are hard
- 2 tablespoons finely shredded coconut

Directions:

1. Finely chop the almonds in a food processor. Blend in the salt, cocoa, oats and flaxseeds until well combined.
2. Next goes in the oil and dates. Blend until well combined. The mixture should come together when you press it. If it crumbles, add more oil and blend. If it is very sticky, add some oats and blend again until well combined.
3. Prepare a baking sheet by lining it with parchment paper.
4. Divide the mixture into 10 equal portions. Shape them into balls. Dredge the balls in coconut, one at a time. Press lightly to adhere. Place the balls on the baking sheet.
5. Chill for an hour. Transfer into an airtight container and refrigerate until use. It can last for 10 - 12 days.

Healthy Matcha Green Tea Fudge Bars

Preparation time: 20 minutes

Cooking time: 0 minutes

Number of servings: 6

Ingredients:

- ¼ cup roasted almond butter
- ¾ teaspoon vanilla crème flavored stevia extract
- ½ cup + 2 tablespoons vanilla brown rice protein powder
- 1 tablespoon matcha powder
- ½ cup + 1 tablespoon unsweetened vanilla almond milk
- ½ teaspoon almond extract
- 1/3 cup oat flour
- A pinch salt

Directions:

1. Prepare a small, square pan by lining it with parchment paper.

2. Add almond butter, stevia, protein powder, matcha powder, milk, almond extract, oat flour and salt into a bowl. Beat with an electric hand mixer until well incorporated and thick, like fudge.

3. Spoon the mixture into the prepared baking pan. Spread it evenly with a spatula. Cover with cling wrap. Make sure that it is tightly covered. Chill for 7 – 8 hours.

4. Cut into 6 equal bars and serve. Store the leftovers in an airtight container in the refrigerator.

Sirtfood Bites

Preparation time: 10 minutes

Cooking time: 0 minutes

Number of servings: 8 – 10

Ingredients:

- ½ cup walnuts
- 4.5 ounces medjool dates, pitted
- ½ tablespoon turmeric powder
- ½ teaspoon vanilla extract
- ½ ounce dark chocolate, chopped
- ½ tablespoon cocoa powder
- ½ tablespoon extra-virgin olive oil
- ½ - 1 tablespoon water

Directions:

1. Add walnuts and dark chocolate into the food processor bowl and pulse until finely powdered.

2. Add dates, turmeric powder, vanilla, cocoa and oil and process until well incorporated.

3. If the mixture sticks together and doesn't crumble, transfer the mixture into a bowl. If not, add ½ tablespoon water and process until well combined. If the mixture does not come together, add a little more water and process until well combined.

4. Divide the mixture into 8 – 10 equal portions and shape into balls. Place the balls in an airtight container and chill until use. It can last for a week.

Dark Chocolate Cherry Energy Bites

Preparation time: 5 minutes

Cooking time: 25 minutes

Number of servings: 7 – 8

Ingredients:

- ½ cup almonds
- ¼ cup dried cherries
- 1/8 teaspoon ground cinnamon
- ¼ cup dark chocolate morsels
- 1 cup pitted dates
- A pinch sea salt

Directions:

1. Place almonds in the food processor and process until chopped into slightly smaller pieces.

2. Add chocolate, cherries, dates, salt and cinnamon and process until the texture you desire is achieved.

3. Transfer into a bowl. Divide the mixture into 7 – 8 equal portions and shape into balls.

4. Transfer into an airtight container and refrigerate until use. It can last for a week.

Sunflower-Coated Cheesy Kale Chips

Preparation time: 1 hour and 15 minutes

Cooking time: 25 minutes

Number of servings: 3

Ingredients:

- 1 large bunch kale, discard hard stems and ribs, torn into bite size pieces

For sunflower coating:

- Salt to taste
- ½ tablespoon lemon juice
- ¼ teaspoon turmeric powder
- A pinch cayenne pepper or to taste
- ½ cup raw sunflower seeds
- 2 tablespoons nutritional yeast or more to taste
- 2 tablespoons water or more if required

Directions:

1. Prepare a large baking sheet by lining it with parchment paper.
2. Place sunflower seeds in a bowl. Pour boiling water over it. Set aside for an hour to soak.
3. Drain and transfer into a blender. Add lemon juice, turmeric, cayenne, nutritional yeast, salt and water and blend until you get smooth texture. Add more salt and cayenne pepper after tasting, if desired.
4. Pour into a large bowl.
5. Place a sheet of parchment paper in a baking sheet.
6. Dry the kale well using a salad spinner. If you do not have a salad spinner, pat dry with paper towels.
7. Add kale into the bowl of sunflower mixture and stir until kale is well coated with the mixture, using your hands.

8. Place kale on the baking sheet. Spread it in a single layer. Use more baking sheets if necessary or bake them in batches.

9. Bake the kale chips in an oven preheated to 225° F, about 20 minutes or until crisp. Stir after about 12 - 15 minutes of baking.

10. Cool completely and serve right away.

Quinoa & Kale Muffins

Preparation time: 10 minutes

Cooking time: 40 minutes

Number of servings: 4

Ingredients:

- Olive oil, to grease
- 2 small cloves garlic, peeled, minced
- 2 large eggs
- 1.75 ounces ground almonds
- 2 tablespoons minced shallot
- A handful kale, discard hard stems and ribs, finely chopped
- 3.5 ounces cooked, leftover quinoa
- Pepper to taste
- 2 – 3 tablespoons crumbled feta cheese
- Salt to taste

To serve:

- ½ ripe avocado, peeled, pitted, mashed
- Chopped chives
- Pepper to taste
- Salt to taste

Directions:

1. Prepare 4 muffin cups by lining it with disposable paper liners. Smear olive oil over the liners.
2. Whisk eggs in a bowl, adding salt and pepper. Stir in shallot, kale, almonds, garlic, quinoa and feta.
3. Divide equally the mixture into the muffin cups.
4. Bake the muffins in an oven preheated to 350° F, for about 20 - 25 minutes.
5. Meanwhile, add avocado, chives, salt and pepper into a bowl and mix well. Cover and set aside for a while.
6. When the muffins are cooked, remove them from the oven and let it cool for a while.
7. Remove the muffin from the cups. Smear avocado mixture on top and serve.

Coffee Gelatin and Mascarpone Cheese

Preparation time: 20 minutes

Cooking time: 15 minutes

Number of servings: 4

Ingredients:

- 4 - 6 sheets natural gelatin
- 8.8 ounces mascarpone cheese
- 2 cups brewed coffee
- Sweetener of your choice to taste
- 4 egg whites

Directions:

1. Soak gelatin sheets in water for a few minutes, until you brew the coffee.
2. Brew coffee like you usually do. Add sweetener and stir. Cool for a while.
3. Discard the water from the bowl of gelatin sheets. Pat the sheets dry.

4. Add gelatin back into the bowl. Pour coffee over it. Chill for a couple of hours.

5. Meanwhile, beat the egg whites until stiff peaks are formed.

6. Mix in the mascarpone cheese. Divide into 4 cups. Pour chilled gelatin coffee over the cheese mixture.

7. Serve.

Key Lime Coconut Energy Bites

Preparation time: 10 minutes

Cooking time: 0 minutes

Number of servings: 3 (2 bites per serving)

Ingredients:

- ¼ cup cashews
- ¼ cup almonds
- Zest of 1 ½ key limes, grated
- Juice of 1 ½ key limes
- ¾ cup pitted dates
- ¼ cup desiccated coconut

Directions:

1. Add the nuts into the food processor bowl and give short pulses until finely chopped.

2. Add dates, lime juice and lime zest and pulse until well combined and the mixture sticks together when pressed.

3. Divide the mixture into 6 equal portions and shape into balls.

4. Dredge the bites in coconut and place in an airtight container. Refrigerate until use. It can last for a week.

Herbed Cheese Ball

Preparation time: 10 minutes

Cooking time: 0 minutes

Number of servings: 8 – 10

Ingredients:

- 2 packages (8 ounces each) cream cheese
- ¼ cup chopped fresh parsley
- 4 teaspoons mixed dried herbs (mixture of parsley, rosemary and thyme)
- ¼ - ½ cup crumbled blue cheese
- 4 teaspoons dried thyme, to garnish
- Assorted crackers to serve (optional)
- 2 tablespoons finely chopped walnuts

Directions:

1. Add cream cheese and blue cheese into a mixing bowl and set aside to soften for about 45 minutes.
2. Beat on low speed with an electric hand mixer until smooth, light and creamy.
3. Add dried herbs and parsley and mix well.
4. Cover the bowl with plastic wrap and chill for 3 – 4 hours or until it can be shaped into a ball.
5. Shape the cheese mixture into one big ball. Place thyme and walnuts on a plate and stir. Dredge the ball in thyme mixture.
6. Cover and chill for at least a couple of hours.
7. Slice and serve as it is or with crackers.

Vegan Tofu "Fish" Sticks

Preparation time: 30 minutes

Cooking time: 40 minutes

Number of servings: 8 – 12

Ingredients:

- 4 blocks firm or extra-firm tofu,
- 4 tablespoons soy sauce
- 2 cups breadcrumbs
- 2 teaspoon lemon pepper
- ½ cup soy milk
- 4 tablespoons lemon juice
- 4 tablespoons crumbled nori seaweed
- Flour, as required
- Salt to taste

Directions:

1. To press tofu: Place tofu over layers of paper towels. Place more towels on top of the tofu.
2. Place something heavy over the tofu. Let it remain like this for 20 minutes. Cut tofu into strips like sticks.
3. Prepare a baking sheet by lining it with parchment paper.
4. Place breadcrumbs in a shallow bowl.
5. Dredge tofu in flour and place on a tray.
6. Combine soy milk, salt, lemon juice and soy sauce in a 2nd shallow bowl.
7. Combine breadcrumbs, lemon pepper and nori in a 3rd shallow bowl.
8. Dunk tofu in soymilk mixture, one at a time. Shake off excess milk mixture and dredge it in breadcrumbs mixture and place on the baking sheet.

Bake tofu in an oven preheated to 375° F, for about 45 minutes or until crisp and

No-Bake Rawies

Preparation time: 10 minutes

Cooking time: 0 minutes

Number of servings: 15

Ingredients:

- 7 ounces pitted dates
- 3 tablespoons cocoa
- ½ teaspoon ground cinnamon
- ½ cup desiccated coconut
- 1/3 cup roasted almonds
- 1 teaspoon vanilla extract

To garnish:

- 15 roasted almonds

Directions:

1. Add dates, cocoa, cinnamon, coconut, almonds and vanilla into the food processor bowl and blend until well combined.
2. Divide the mixture into 15 equal portions and shape into balls.
3. Place an almond on each ball and press to adhere and flatten the ball.
4. Place in an airtight container and refrigerate until use. It can last for 15 days.

Tomato Bruschetta

Preparation time: 10 minutes

Cooking time: 15 minutes

Number of servings: 8

Ingredients:

- 1 ½ pounds fresh tomatoes, diced
- 6 cloves garlic, finely chopped
- 4 tablespoons extra- virgin olive oil

- Pepper to taste
- Salt to taste
- 1 medium onion, finely chopped
- 2 tablespoons chopped fresh basil
- 2 tablespoons chopped fresh parsley

Directions:

1. Add tomatoes, garlic, oil, seasonings, onion, and herbs into a bowl and toss well.
2. Cover and chill for a couple of hours.
3. Toss well and serve as it is or over toasted whole-wheat baguette slices.

Strawberry and Coconut Ice-Blocks

Preparation time: 5 minutes

Cooking time: 0 minutes

Number of servings: 6

Ingredients:

- 1 ½ cups chopped strawberries
- Coconut water, as required

Directions:

1. Take 6 Popsicle molds and add ¼ cup strawberries into each.
2. Pour enough coconut water to fill up the molds up to slightly more than ¾. Insert the Popsicle sticks and freeze until firm.
3. Dip the Popsicle molds in warm water for about 15 seconds. Remove from the molds and serve.

Berry Smoothie Ice-Blocks

Preparation time: 5 minutes

Cooking time: 0 minutes

Number of servings: 12

Ingredients:

- 12 strawberries, halved
- ½ cup frozen blueberries
- ½ cup frozen raspberries
- 1 1/3 cups orange juice

Directions:

1. Add orange juice and all the berries into a blender.
2. Blitz until smooth.
3. Pour into Popsicle molds. Insert the Popsicle sticks and freeze until firm.
4. Dip the Popsicle molds in warm water for about 15 seconds. Remove from the molds and serve.

Superfood Trail Mix

Preparation time: 5 minutes

Cooking time: 0 minutes

Number of servings: 16

Ingredients:

- 1 cup whole almonds
- 1 cup whole pistachios
- 1 cup halved walnuts
- 1 cup whole Brazil nuts
- 1 cup dried blueberries
- 1 cup goji berries
- 1 cup dark chocolate chunks or cacao nibs
- ½ cup coconut chips, roasted

Directions:

1. Mix all the nuts, berries, chocolate chips and coconut chips into an airtight container.

2. Store on your countertop. It can last for 2 weeks.

Chapter 8: Vegetarian

Vegetable Omelet

Preparation time: 6 – 8 minutes

Cooking time: 10 – 12 minutes

Number of servings: 2

Ingredients:

- 4 eggs, preferably
- 1 small onion, chopped
- Pepper to taste
- 2 handfuls fresh kale leaves, discard hard stems and ribs or use baby kale, chopped
- 4 tablespoons olive oil, divided
- 1 medium red bell pepper, chopped
- Salt to taste

Directions:

1. Place a skillet over medium-high flame. Add 2 tablespoons of olive oil. When the oil is heated, add onion and bell pepper and cook for a couple of minutes. Stir in the kale and cook for another couple of minutes.

2. Turn off the heat. Transfer the vegetable mixture into a bowl.

3. Add eggs into another bowl and beat well.
4. Place the pan over medium flame.
5. Add 1 tablespoon oil and let it heat.
6. Pour half the eggs into the pan. Swirl the pan to spread the egg. When the omelet is slightly cooked, spread half the vegetable mixture on one half of the omelet. Fold the other half of the omelet over the filling.
7. Carefully remove the omelet onto a plate and serve right away.
8. Repeat steps 5 – 7 and make the other omelet.

Kale Stir Fry with Crispy Curried Tofu

Preparation time: 15 minutes

Cooking time: 15 minutes

Number of servings: 4

Ingredients:

For crispy curried tofu:

- 2 blocks (7 ounces each) firm tofu, cut into 1 inch cubes
- 2 tablespoons soy sauce
- 3 teaspoons curry powder
- ½ red cabbage, thinly sliced
- Olive oil as required

For stir-fry:

- 8 large kale leaves, discard hard stems and ribs, thinly sliced
- 2 cloves garlic, peeled, minced
- 4 tablespoons soy sauce
- 2 carrots, thinly sliced
- 2 inches piece fresh ginger, peeled, minced
- 4 portions whole-wheat noodles
- Olive oil, as required

Directions:

1. Combine 1 ½ teaspoons curry powder and soy sauce in a bowl.
2. Stir in the tofu. Make sure that tofu is well coated with the sauce mixture. Cover and set aside for 15 minutes.
3. Follow the directions on the package and cook the noodles.
4. Place 2 pans with a little oil in each, over medium flame on 2 different burners on your stovetop.
5. Add tofu into one pan and cook until golden brown all over. Stir frequently. Remove the tofu with a slotted spoon and place on a plate lined with paper towels.
6. Simultaneously, add ginger and garlic into the other pan and cook for a few seconds until aromatic.
7. Stir in kale and cabbage, cooking until slightly limp.
8. Stir in carrot and soy sauce and cook for a couple of minutes.
9. Divide noodles into 4 plates. Divide the stir fry vegetables over the noodles. Scatter tofu on top and serve right away.

Kale, Pumpkin Seed and Potato One Pot Dinner

Preparation time: 15 minutes

Cooking time: 15 minutes

Number of servings: 8

Ingredients:

- 1 pound potatoes, peeled, cut into bite size cubes
- 2 green bell peppers, chopped into 1 inch square pieces
- 2 orange bell peppers, chopped into 1 inch square pieces
- 2 large eggplants, sliced
- 2 large red onions, sliced
- 7 ounces curly kale, sliced
- 10.5 ounces baby spinach
- 4 large carrots, cut into matchsticks

- 1 can (28 ounces) plum tomatoes
- ½ cup olive oil
- 2 vegetable stock cubes
- ¼ cup ground pumpkin seeds
- 2 teaspoons sea salt or to taste

Directions:

1. Blend the plum tomatoes in a blender until smooth.
2. Season eggplant with some salt and immerse in a bowl of hot water for a couple of minutes. Rinse well.
3. Place a Dutch oven over medium flame. Add oil. When the oil is heated, add potatoes and cook for 8 - 10 minutes, stirring occasionally.
4. Stir in the carrots and eggplant and cook for about 2 minutes. Stir in the bell peppers, pumpkin seeds and plum tomatoes. Stir occasionally and cook for about 6 - 7 minutes.
5. Crumble the vegetable stock cubes and add into the pot along with salt to taste. Cook covered, on low heat until the potatoes are fork tender. Stir occasionally.
6. Stir in the kale and cook for 3 - 4 minutes. Remove from heat.
7. Stir in the spinach and keep the pot covered.
8. Serve hot.

Springtime Buckwheat Risotto

Preparation time: 8 - 9 hours

Cooking time: 20 - 25 minutes

Number of servings: 2

Ingredients:

- ½ cup vegetable stock
- ½ big bunch asparagus, halved, trim the tough ends
- ½ small red onion, finely chopped
- ½ tablespoon dried Italian herbs

- Juice of ½ lemon
- Zest of ½ lemon, grated
- 1 tablespoon nutritional yeast
- Pepper to taste
- 1 cup chopped spinach
- Extra-virgin olive oil, to drizzle
- 1 tablespoon olive oil
- 1 clove garlic, peeled, minced
- 4.4 ounces buckwheat, soaked in water overnight, drained, rinsed
- ½ tablespoon apple cider vinegar
- ¼ cup frozen or fresh peas, thaw if frozen
- 1 cup mixture of fresh parsley, basil and oregano + extra to garnish
- Salt to taste

Directions:

1. Boil stock in a saucepan. Lower the heat and let it simmer.
2. Place a pan over medium flame. Add ½ tablespoon of oil. When the oil is heated, add asparagus and cook until crisp and tender.
3. Take out the asparagus from the pan and place it on a plate.
4. Add ½ tablespoon oil into the pan. Once oil is heated, add onion and garlic and sauté until onion turns translucent.
5. Stir in the buckwheat, apple cider vinegar, dried herbs and lemon juice.
6. Once well, combined, add the simmering stock and mix well. When the stock is absorbed, add a little more stock and repeat this process of adding stock until all of it is added, making sure that the stock is absorbed each time, before adding more stock.
7. When buckwheat is well cooked, add spinach and peas and mix well. Cook for a couple of minutes.
8. Add fresh herbs, nutritional yeast, lemon zest, pepper and salt. Mix well.

9. To serve: Divide risotto into bowls. Place asparagus on top. Trickle some extra-virgin olive oil on top. Garnish with some fresh herbs and serve.

Miso & Sesame Glazed Tofu Stir-Fry

Preparation time: 25 minutes

Cooking time: 25 – 30 minutes

Number of servings: 4

Ingredients:

- 4 tablespoons mirin
- 1.1 pounds tofu, cut into slabs and then into triangles
- 2 red onions, thinly sliced
- 4 bird's eye chili, deseeded if desired, finely chopped
- 4 teaspoons minced ginger
- 8 teaspoons sesame seeds
- 2 cups water
- 8 teaspoons extra-virgin olive oil
- 4 tablespoons brown miso paste
- 2 sticks celery, trimmed, finely chopped
- 2 courgettes, thinly sliced
- 4 cloves garlic, peeled, finely chopped
- 2 ½ cups chopped kale
- 1 cup buckwheat groats or buckwheat noodles
- 4 teaspoons turmeric powder
- 4 teaspoons soy sauce or tamari

Directions:

1. Prepare a roasting pan by lining it with parchment paper.

2. Combine miso and mirin in a large bowl. Add tofu and stir until tofu is well coated with the mixture. Let it marinate for 20 minutes.

3. Transfer the tofu into the roasting pan and spread it evenly. Scatter sesame seeds over the tofu.

4. Bake tofu in an oven preheated to 400° F, for about 15 to 20 minutes brown.

5. Meanwhile, boil water in a saucepan with turmeric and salt, over high flame.

6. As the water begins to boil, stir in the buckwheat and cook until it comes to a boil.

7. Lower the heat and cook covered until dry. Turn off the heat and set aside.

8. If you are using buckwheat noodles, cook the noodles following the directions on the package and add turmeric in step 11.

9. 5 minutes before removing the tofu from the oven, place a pan over medium – high flame.

10. Add oil and let it heat. Add onion and cook for a minute.

11. Stir in ginger, garlic, celery, courgette and bird's eye chili and mix well. Once the mixture turns fragrant (in about a minute), lower the flame to medium flame. Cook until vegetables are tender.

12. Stir in kale and tamari and cook until kale wilts.

13. Serve tofu with vegetables and buckwheat.

Veggie Sandwich

Preparation time: 15 minutes

Cooking time: 0 minutes

Number of servings: 2

Ingredients:

- 4 slices whole grain bread
- 4 Romaine lettuce leaves
- ½ cup thinly sliced red bell peppers
- 1 medium red onion, thinly sliced into rounds
- 1 small cucumber, thinly sliced
- 4 teaspoons pumpkin seeds
- Salt to taste
- 4 tablespoons hummus

- ½ cup microgreens
- 2 tablespoons shredded carrots
- ½ large apple, cored, thinly sliced
- 4 teaspoons pumpkin seeds
- Pepper to taste

Directions:

1. Smear hummus on one side of each of the bread slices.
2. Place 2 lettuce leaves on 2 of the bread slices.
3. Place onion slices, cucumber slices, red bell pepper slices and apple over the lettuce. Scatter microgreens, carrots and pumpkin seeds. Place a lettuce leaf on top of each stack.
4. Cover with the remaining 2 bread slices, with the hummus side facing down.

Ricotta Sandwiches with Carrots, Kale and Walnut-Parsley Pesto

Preparation time: 20 - 25 minutes

Cooking time: 30 minutes

Number of servings: 4

Ingredients:

For carrots:

- 2 cups thinly sliced carrots
- tablespoon maple syrup
- - 4 tablespoons olive oil
- Salt to taste

For ricotta:

- 2 cups ricotta
- Salt to taste
- 1 teaspoon grated lemon zest
- Chili flakes, to taste

For vinaigrette:

- ½ cup olive oil
- ½ cup canola oil
- ½ cup maple syrup
- ½ cup sherry vinegar
- 2 small shallots, finely minced

For walnut parsley pesto:

- 2 bunches parsley
- 2 cups parmesan cheese
- 2 tablespoons lemon juice
- 2/3 cup walnuts, toast if necessary
- Olive oil, as required
- Salt to taste

To serve:

- 4 handfuls kale leaves, torn, discard
- 8 slices multi-grain bread

Directions:

1. To roast carrots: Combine carrots, salt, maple syrup and oil on a baking sheet lined with parchment paper and spread it evenly, in a single layer.

2. Bake carrots in an oven preheated to 360° F, for about 25 to 30 minutes or until tender.

3. For ricotta: Combine lemon zest, ricotta, chili flakes and salt in a bowl. Cover and set aside in the refrigerator until use.

4. For pesto: add walnuts, lemon juice and parsley into the food processor bowl and process until well combined.

5. With the food processor running, pour oil in a thin drizzle until smooth and the consistency you desire is achieved.

6. Pour into a bowl and refrigerate until use.

7. For vinaigrette: Add vinegar, maple syrup, oil and shallot in a small glass jar. Fasten the lid and shake the jar vigorously until well combined. Refrigerate until use.

8. To serve: Toast the bread slices to the desired doneness.

9. Add kale into a bowl and pour required amount of dressing over it. Refrigerate the remaining and use in some salads.

10. Spread pesto on 4 of the bread slices and set it aside.

11. Spread a generous amount of ricotta on the other 4 slices of bread. Place carrot slices over it. Spread kale over the carrot slices.

12. Cover with the remaining bread slices, with the pesto side facing down.

13. Cut into desired shape and serve.

Squash and Kale Gratin Casserole

Preparation time: 15 minutes

Cooking time: 20 minutes

Number of servings: 4

Ingredients:

- 2 cups thinly sliced butternut squash, peeled, deseeded, very thinly sliced
- 1 teaspoon olive oil
- 4 cups roughly chopped kale
- ½ cup roughly chopped red onion
- ¼ cup grated gruyere cheese
- A pinch ground nutmeg
- 3 cloves garlic, minced
- Kosher salt to taste
- 1/3 cup whole milk or coconut milk, divided
- Pepper to taste
- 6 tablespoons water or more if required
- ¼ teaspoon ground cumin
- A pinch cayenne pepper
- 1 tablespoon cornstarch or all-purpose flour
- ½ cup whole-wheat panko breadcrumbs
- ½ teaspoon butter

Directions:

1. Prepare a small casserole dish by spraying some cooking spray.
2. Place a nonstick pan over medium-high flame. Add oil. When the oil is heated, add onion and garlic and cook until golden. Add kale and cook until it wilts. Turn off the heat.
3. Add cornstarch and a tablespoon of milk in a bowl. Pour remaining milk into a saucepan. Place the saucepan over low heat. When the milk is heated, add the flour mixture and stir constantly until thick.
4. Stir in cheese, salt and all the spices. Cook until the cheese melts. Turn off the heat. Pour the sauce into the pan of kale and mix well.
5. Place a layer of squash slices in the casserole dish. Spread half the kale mixture over the squash.
6. Repeat the previous step once more.
7. Sprinkle breadcrumbs on top. Keep the dish covered with foil.
8. Bake in a preheated oven at 350° F, for about 30-40 minutes or until light brown on top.
9. Remove from the oven and cool slightly before serving.

Three-Bean Chili with Spring Pesto

Preparation time: 10 minutes

Cooking time: 15 minutes

Number of servings: 8

Ingredients:

- ½ cup + 2 tablespoons extra- virgin olive oil, divided
- 2 carrots, diced
- Pepper to taste
- 1 large red onion, chopped
- 2 cans (15.5 ounces each) diced tomatoes with its liquid
- 2 cans (15.5 ounces each) chickpeas, rinsed, drained

- 2 cans (15.5 ounces each) kidney beans, rinsed, drained
- 2 cans (15.5 ounces each) cannellini beans, rinsed, drained
- 6 tablespoons chopped pine nuts
- 2 small cloves garlic, peeled, minced
- ½ cup fresh flat leaf parsley, chopped
- Salt to taste
- 4 cups water
- Crusty bread to serve (optional)

Directions:

1. Place a soup pot over medium-high flame. Add 2 tablespoons oil and wait until it is heated.

2. Stir in the onions and carrots and sauté until onions are translucent.

3. Add tomatoes, water, salt, pepper, chickpeas, kidney beans and cannellini beans and stir. Heat thoroughly.

4. To make spring pesto: In a small bowl, mix garlic, ½ cup oil, salt, pepper, pine nuts and parsley.

5. Serve soup in bowls. Divide the spring pesto among the bowls and serve with crusty bread if desired.

Apple Glazed Vegetable & Edamame Stir-Fry

Preparation time: 15 minutes

Cooking time: 30 minutes

Number of servings: 8

Ingredients:

- 8 cups cubed vegetables of your choice like squash, bell peppers, celery, sweet potato, potato or any favorite veggie of your choice
- 1 large red onion, cut into 1 inch square pieces, separate the layers
- 1 cup water

- 1 teaspoon Old Bay seasoning
- ½ cup brown (optional)
- 1 cup applesauce
- 2 teaspoons ground ginger
- 6 tablespoons rice wine vinegar or apple cider vinegar
- 4 tablespoons soy sauce or hoisin sauce
- 1 cup cooked edamame beans
- Salt to taste
- ½ teaspoon red pepper flakes
- 1 teaspoon minced garlic
- Pepper to taste
- Cooking spray

Directions:

1. Place a large nonstick pan or wok over high flame and let the pan heat. Grease the pan by spraying some cooking spray.

2. Add onion and garlic and cook for a couple of minutes. Add all the vegetables except edamame and mix well. Cook covered, until tender.

3. Add water, seasonings, spices, applesauce, vinegar and soy sauce into a bowl and stir. Pour into the pan and mix until well coated.

4. Lower the heat to medium-low and cook until tender.

5. Add edamame and mix well. Heat thoroughly and serve.

Kale, Edamame and Tofu Curry

Preparation time: 15 minutes

Cooking time: 20 minutes

Number of servings: 8

Ingredients:

- 2 tablespoons olive oil
- 8 cloves garlic, peeled, grated
- 2 bird's eye chili, deseeded, thinly sliced

- ½ teaspoon cayenne pepper
- 1 teaspoon ground cumin
- 1 teaspoon turmeric powder
- 2 teaspoons paprika
- 2 teaspoons salt or to taste
- 1.1 pounds dry red lentils, rinsed
- 3.5 ounces frozen edamame beans
- 4 tomatoes, chopped
- 2 bunches kale, discard hard stems and ribs, torn
- 8 cups boiling water
- 14 ounces firm tofu, cubed
- Juice of 2 limes

Directions:

1. Place a heavy pot over medium-low flame. Add oil. When the oil is heated, add onions and cook until slightly soft. Stir in ginger, garlic and chili and cook for a few seconds until aromatic.

2. Stir in the spices and salt. Cook for a few more seconds and add red lentils.

3. Add boiling water and cook for 10 minutes. Lower the heat and cook covered until lentils are tender.

4. Stir in edamame, tomatoes and tofu. Cook until tomatoes are soft. Stir in lime juice and kale and cook until kale wilts.

5. Serve hot over hot cooked rice or quinoa or buckwheat.

Shirataki Noodles with Kale and Chickpeas

Preparation time: 10 minutes

Cooking time: 10 minutes

Number of servings: 2

Ingredients:

- 1 tablespoon extra-virgin olive oil
- ½ large bunch kale, discard hard stems and ribs

- 1 package (8 ounces) shirataki noodles
- Salt to taste
- 2 cloves garlic, peeled, minced
- Freshly ground pepper to taste
- ½ can (from a 15 ounces can) chickpeas, rinsed, drained
- 2 ounces shiitake mushrooms, thickly sliced
- 2 tablespoons chopped parsley
- ¼ cup marinara sauce

Directions:

1. Place a cast iron skillet over medium flame. Add oil and let it heat. Once oil is heated, add garlic and cook for a few seconds until fragrant.

2. Add kale and cook for a few minutes until it goes limp.

3. Stir in chickpeas, mushrooms, shirataki noodles and marinara sauce and heat thoroughly. Add salt and pepper and toss well.

4. Sprinkle parsley on top and serve.

Chapter 9: Dinner

Spiced Cauliflower Couscous with Chicken

Preparation time: 15 minutes

Cooking time: 20 minutes

Number of servings: 2

Ingredients:

- 2 cups roughly chopped cauliflower florets
- A handful fresh flat-leaf parsley
- 2 cloves garlic, finely chopped
- ½ cup finely chopped red onions
- 2 teaspoons finely chopped ginger
- 1/3 cup sun-dried tomatoes
- 2 tablespoons capers
- 2 chicken breasts
- 4 teaspoons turmeric powder
- ½ cup finely diced carrots
- 2 bird's eye chilies, finely chopped
- 4 tablespoons extra-virgin olive oil
- Juice of a lemon

Directions:

1. You can chop the cauliflower in a food processor.
2. Place a pan over medium - high flame. Add 2 tablespoons oil. When the oil is heated, add ginger, garlic and chili and cook for a few seconds until fragrant.
3. Stir in turmeric and cook for 5 - 8 seconds. Stir in the carrots and cauliflower and cook for about 2 minutes. Turn off the heat.
4. Transfer into a bowl. Add tomatoes and parsley and stir. Keep warm.
5. Add remaining oil into the pan and let it heat. Place chicken in the pan and cook for about 6 minutes. Turn the chicken over and cook for 5 - 6 minutes or until well-cooked inside.
6. Stir in capers, lemon juice and a sprinkle of water.
7. Add cauliflower and carrot mixture and toss well.
8. Serve.

Chicken Noodles

Preparation time: 10 minutes

Cooking time: 30 minutes

Number of servings: 8 - 10

Ingredients:

- 16 ounces buckwheat noodles
- 2 yellow bell peppers, chopped into ½ inch squares
- 6 cloves garlic, chopped
- 2 tablespoons olive oil
- 6 cups tomato sauce
- 2 tablespoons fresh basil, chopped or 2 teaspoons dry basil
- 2 tablespoons fresh parsley, chopped or 2 teaspoons dried parsley
- Pepper to taste
- 2 pounds skinless, boneless chicken breast, cut into strips
- 1 large red onion, chopped into ½ inch squares, separate the layers

- Salt to taste

Directions:

1. Follow the directions on the package and cook the buckwheat noodles.
2. Place a large skillet over medium flame. Add oil and wait for the oil to heat. Add chicken strips and spread it all over the pan and cook undisturbed, until the underside is cooked. Flip sides and cook the other side, undisturbed.
3. Add the vegetables and mix well. Cook until the vegetables are tender. Add tomato sauce and cook for 7-8 minutes.
4. Add noodles and toss well.
5. Serve hot.

Aromatic Chicken Breast with Kale, Red Onion and Salsa

Preparation time: 10 minutes

Cooking time: 20 minutes

Number of servings: 2

Ingredients:

- ounces skinless, boneless chicken breasts
- 2 teaspoons lemon juice
- ounces kale leaves, chopped
- 2 teaspoons minced fresh ginger
- 4 teaspoons turmeric powder
- 2 tablespoons extra-virgin olive oil
- medium red onion, sliced
- ounces buckwheat groats

For salsa:

- tomatoes, finely chopped
- chili, sliced
- tablespoon capers

- teaspoons lemon juice
- ¼ cup minced parsley
- Salt to taste

Directions;

- To make salsa: Combine tomatoes, chili, capers, lemon juice, parsley and salt into a bowl and toss well. Cover and set aside for a while for the flavors to set in.
- Sprinkle 2 teaspoons turmeric powder over the chicken. Drizzle lemon juice and a little over it.
- Place an ovenproof pan over medium flame. Add a little oil. When the oil is heated, add chicken and cook until light golden brown all over.
- Shift the pan into an oven preheated to 450° F and bake for about 20 minutes or well-cooked inside.
- Remove the pan from the oven and tent loosely with foil.
- Meanwhile, steam kale for 5 minutes in the steaming equipment you have.
- Also cook the buckwheat noodles following the directions on the package, adding remaining turmeric while cooking.
- Place a skillet over medium flame. Add some oil. When the oil is heated, add onion and ginger and cook until slightly tender.
- Stir in kale and cook for a minute.
- Serve chicken with vegetables with salsa on the side.

Chicken Butternut Squash Pasta

Preparation time: 10 minutes

Cooking time: 30 – 40 minutes

Number of servings: 2

Ingredients:

- ½ pound ground chicken
- tablespoon balsamic vinegar
- ½ tablespoon olive oil, divided

- ½ cups whole wheat pasta
- Pepper to taste
- fresh basil leaves, thinly sliced
- tablespoons chopped walnuts
- Salt to taste
- ½ cups cubed butternut squash, cut into ½" cubes
- ounces goat's cheese, crumbled
- ½ teaspoon garlic, minced
- 1/8 teaspoon ground nutmeg

Directions:

1 Place butternut squash on a baking sheet. Drizzle 1 tablespoon oil and sprinkle salt and pepper over the squash. Toss well.

2 Bake squash in an oven preheated to 400° F, for about 30 minutes or until tender.

3 Cook the pasta following the directions on the package.

4 Place a skillet over medium heat. Add ½ tablespoon oil and wait for it to heat. Add garlic and cook until light brown, stirring often.

5 Add chicken and cook until the chicken is not pink anymore.

6 Stir in walnuts, nutmeg and vinegar.

7 Cook on low heat for 1 – 2 minutes.

8 Serve chicken over pasta.

9 Scatter butternut squash and goat's cheese. Sprinkle basil on top.

10 Serve.

Chicken Marsala

Preparation time: 10 minutes

Cooking time: 30 – 40 minutes

Number of servings: 8

Ingredients:

- 8 boneless, skinless chicken breasts (6 ounces each)
- 20 ounces cremini mushrooms, sliced
- 2 cloves garlic, peeled, sliced
- 1 cup marsala wine
- 6 tablespoons flour
- 2 large shallots, chopped
- Salt to taste
- 1 cup chicken broth
- Freshly ground pepper to taste
- 4 - 5 tablespoons olive oil
- 2 tablespoons chopped parsley
- Sautéed spinach to serve

Directions:

1. Place the chicken breasts between 2 sheets of plastic wrap and pound with a meat mallet until ½ inch in thickness.

2. Sprinkle salt and pepper over the chicken. Sprinkle flour over the chicken.

3. Place a large skillet over medium flame. Add about a tablespoon of oil and swirl the pan to spread the oil.

4. Place as many chicken pieces as possible in the pan. Sear the chicken on both the sides until golden brown. Remove the chicken from the pan placed on a plate using a slotted spoon.

5. Cook the remaining chicken in the same way, adding more oil if required.

6. Add 2 tablespoons oil into the skillet. When the oil is heated, add mushrooms and cook until brown.

7. Stir in garlic and shallots. Add salt and pepper to taste and stir-fry for 1 - 2 minutes.

8. Add wine, broth and chicken along with the released juice and cook until the liquid in the pan is half its original quantity.

9. Garnish with parsley and serve along with sautéed spinach or any other sautéed greens of your choice.

Chicken Skewers with Satay Sauce

Preparation time: 60 minutes

Cooking time: 30 minutes

Number of servings: 2

Ingredients:

For chicken:

- 10.5 ounces chicken breasts, chopped into chunks
- 1 teaspoon extra-virgin olive oil
- A handful kale leaves, discard stems and ribs, sliced
- 2 teaspoons turmeric powder

For satay sauce:

- 2 teaspoons extra-virgin olive oil
- 1 medium red onion, diced
- 2 stalks celery, sliced
- 2 teaspoons curry powder
- ½ cup chicken stock
- 2 tablespoons walnut butter or peanut butter
- 1 ¼ cups coconut milk
- 2 teaspoons turmeric powder
- 2 cloves garlic, peeled, chopped
- Salt to taste
- A handful fresh cilantro, chopped

To serve:

- 8 walnut halves, chopped, to garnish
- 3.5 ounces buckwheat

Directions:

1 Combine olive oil and turmeric powder in a bowl. Add chicken and stir until chicken is well coated with the mixture. Cover and set aside for about an hour.

2 Meanwhile, follow the directions on the package and cook the buckwheat. Add kale and celery during the last 5 minutes of cooking.

3 Set up your grill and preheat it to high.

4 To make satay sauce: Place a pan over medium flame. Add oil and let it heat. Add onion and garlic and cook for a few minutes until onions turn pink.

5 Stir in turmeric and curry powder and cook for a few more seconds.

6 Pour stock and coconut milk and mix well. When the mixture comes to a boil, stir in the walnut butter. Mix until well combined.

7 Lower the heat and simmer until sauce is thick. Turn off the heat. Add cilantro and stir.

8 While the sauce is thickening, insert the chicken on 2 skewers.

9 Grill the chicken for 10 minutes. Turn the skewers every 3 - 4 minutes.

10 Place the skewers on individual serving plates.

11 Drizzle sauce over the skewers. Scatter walnuts on top and serve.

Turkey Steak with Spicy Cauliflower Couscous

Preparation time: 10 minutes

Cooking time: 15 - 18 minutes

Number of servings: 2 - 3

Ingredients:

- 2 - 3 turkey steaks
- ½ red onion, chopped
- tablespoon ground turmeric
- Juice of ½ lemon
- Olive oil, as required
- ½ cauliflower, chopped to couscous like texture
- Bird's eye chili, chopped
- Salt to taste
- ½ cup chopped parsley

- clove garlic, peeled, minced
- Pepper to taste

Directions:

1 Sprinkle salt, pepper and lemon juice over the steaks.

2 Place a pan over medium flame. Add a little oil and let it heat. Add onion, garlic and chili and cook until slightly pink.

3 Stir in the turmeric and cauliflower. Heat thoroughly. Turn off the heat. Stir in parsley.

4 Cook the steaks on a preheated grill or in a grill pan.

5 Divide cauliflower couscous into 2 - 3 plates. Top each with a steak and serve.

Turkey Apple Burgers

Preparation time: 15 minutes

Cooking time: 8 - 10 minutes

Number of servings: 2

Ingredients:

- 1 green apple, cored, peeled, halved
- A handful fresh thyme or sage, minced
- Pepper to taste
- ½ teaspoon onion powder
- ¼ teaspoon garlic powder
- Salt to taste
- 1 teaspoon olive oil
- ½ pound 93% lean ground turkey
- Whole-wheat burger buns or lettuce cups to serve
-

Directions:

1 Grate one half of the apple and cut the other half into thin slices.

2 Combine grated apple, spices, salt, sage and turkey in a bowl and mix well.

3 Make 2 equal portions of the mixture. Shape into patties.

4 Place a skillet over medium flame. Brush oil on both the sides of the patties and place in the pan.

5 Cook until the underside is brown. Turn the burgers over and cook the other side until brown.

6 Serve burgers over buns or lettuce cups. Place sliced apples on top of the burgers and serve.

Turkey Sandwiches with Apple and Walnut Mayo

Preparation time: 15 minutes

Cooking time: 4 minutes

Number of servings: 2

Ingredients:

<u>For walnut mayonnaise:</u>

- 2 tablespoons finely chopped walnuts
- 3 - 4 tablespoons mayonnaise
- ½ tablespoon Dijon mustard
- ½ tablespoon chopped, fresh parsley

<u>For sandwich:</u>

- 4 slices whole-wheat bread
- ½ green apple, peeled, cored, cut into thin slices
- Cooked, sliced turkey, as required
- A handful rocket

Directions:

1 To make walnut mayonnaise: Combine walnuts, mayonnaise, mustard and parsley in a bowl.

2 Smear walnut mayonnaise on one side of the bread slices.

3 Place arugula on 2 bread slices, on the mayo side. Place turkey slices over it followed by apple slices.

4 Complete the sandwich by covering with remaining bread slices, with mayo side facing down.

5 Cut into desired shape and serve.

Sautéed Turkey with Tomatoes and Cilantro

Preparation time: 10 minutes

Cooking time: 15 minutes

Number of servings: 2 - 3

Ingredients:

- ½ pound lean ground turkey
- ½ cup chopped yellow or red onion
- Pepper to taste
- 1 teaspoon olive oil
- 1 jalapeño or to taste, chopped
- ½ tablespoon minced garlic
- ¼ cup chopped tomatoes
- ¼ teaspoon ground cumin
- 2 teaspoons red pepper flakes
- ½ cup chopped fresh cilantro
- Salt to taste
- A handful parsley leaves

Directions:

1 Place a skillet over medium flame. Add oil and wait for it to heat. Add garlic and sauté for about a minute until light brown.

2 Stir in onions, tomatoes, jalapeño, parsley and red pepper flakes and cook for 4-5 minutes.

3 Stir in the turkey and cook until brown, breaking the turkey as it cooks.

4 Add cilantro, salt and pepper and stir.

5 Serve hot.

Steak with Spicy Chimichurri Sauce

Preparation time: 15 minutes

Cooking time: 16 – 20 minutes

Number of servings: 3

Ingredients:

- pound sirloin steak
- ¼ teaspoon pepper or to taste
- ¼ teaspoon garlic powder
- Salt to taste
- ¼ teaspoon ground cumin

For chimichurri sauce:

- A handful fresh parsley, finely chopped
- tablespoon finely chopped shallot
- A handful kale and spring mix, finely chopped
- ¼ cup olive oil
- 1/8 teaspoon salt or to taste
- cloves garlic, peeled, minced
- ½ teaspoon honey
- ¼ teaspoon crushed red pepper flakes

Directions:

1 To make chimichurri sauce: Add greens, shallot, salt, honey and red pepper flakes into a bowl and mix well. Cover and set aside for a few minutes.

2 Meanwhile, set up your grill and preheat it to medium-high.

3 Sprinkle salt and spices all over the steak and rub it well into it.

4 Place the steak on the grill and cook for 8 minutes. Flip the steak and cook for 8 minutes for medium – rare or to the desired doneness.

5 Remove the steak from the grill and cover with foil and let it sit for 15 minutes.

6 Cut into slices and divide into plates. Spread chimichurri sauce on top and serve.

Chargrilled Beef with Red Wine Jus, Onion Rings, Garlic Kale and Herb Roasted Potatoes

Preparation time: 10 minutes

Cooking time: 1 hour and 30 minutes

Number of servings: 2

Ingredients:

- 7 ounces potatoes, peeled, cut into 1 inch cubes
- A handful fresh parsley, chopped
- ½ ounce kale leaves, chopped, discard hard stems and ribs
- 2 beef fillet steaks (4 – 5 ounces each) or 1 inch thick sirloin steak
- ¼ cup beef stock
- Salt to taste
- ½ teaspoons cornstarch mixed with 2 tablespoons water
- ½ tablespoons extra-virgin olive oil
- medium red onion, cut into thin rings
- cloves garlic, finely chopped
- Pepper to taste
- tablespoons red wine
- 2 teaspoons tomato puree

Directions:

1. Boil water in a saucepan over high flame. Add potatoes and let it come to a rolling boil. Cook for 4 minutes. Drain in a colander.

2. Transfer the potatoes into a baking dish. Drizzle a tablespoon of oil over the potatoes and toss well. Spread it evenly.

3. Bake in an oven preheated to 440° F, for about 30 – 40 minutes. Stir the potatoes at intervals of 10 minutes.

4. Transfer into a bowl. Add parsley and toss well.

5. Place a skillet over medium flame. Add ½ tablespoon oil. When the oil is heated, add onion and cook until golden brown. Transfer into a bowl.

6. Steam kale in the steaming equipment you have.

7. Add ½ tablespoon oil into the skillet. Add garlic and cook for a few seconds until fragrant. Stir in the kale and cook for a couple of minutes, until it turns slightly limp. Turn off the heat. Cover and set aside.

8. Place an ovenproof pan over high-high flame. Add remaining oil and wait for the oil to heat. Once the oil is heated, add steaks and coat it with oil, on both the sides. Cook for 3 to 4 minutes on each side. Turn off the heat.

9. Shift the saucepan into an oven preheated to 440° F, and roast until the meat is cooked to the desired doneness.

10. Take out the pan from the oven. Set the meat aside on a plate.

11. Pour red wine into the same pan. Deglaze the pan. Place the pan over high flame. Cook until the wine is half its original quantity.

12. Stir in stock, tomato puree, and let it come to a boil.

13. Stir in the corn flour mixture. Keep stirring until thick. Pour any cooked juices of the steak into the pan.

14. Serve steak with potatoes, kale, wine sauce and onions.

Orecchiette with Sausage and Chicory

Preparation time: 10 minutes

Cooking time: 20 – 25 minutes

Number of servings: 3

Ingredients:

- ½ pound Orecchiette
- ½ pound sweet Italian sausage, discard casings
- ¼ teaspoon crushed red pepper
- Salt to taste
- 2 tablespoons grated pecorino + extra to garnish
- 2 tablespoons extra-virgin olive oil
- 1 clove garlic, peeled, thinly sliced
- ½ pound chicory or escarole, chopped
- ½ cup chicken stock

- A handful fresh mint leaves, chopped

Directions:

1. Cook pasta following the directions on the package, adding salt while cooking.

2. Place a large skillet over medium flame. Add a tablespoon of oil and let it heat.

3. Once oil is heated, add sausage and cook until brown. Break it while it cooks.

4. Remove sausage with a slotted spoon and place on a plate.

5. Add a tablespoon of oil. When the oil is heated, add garlic and red pepper and stir for a few seconds until you get a nice aroma.

6. Stir in chicory and salt and cook covered, until they turn limp. It should take a couple of minutes.

7. Uncover and continue cooking until tender.

8. Add pasta, sausage, cheese and stock and cook until the sauce is slightly thick. Add mint and stir.

9. Serve hot.

Chili Con Carne

Preparation time: 15 minutes

Cooking time: 1 hour and 30 minutes

Number of servings: 8

Ingredients:

- 2 red onions, finely chopped
- 4 bird's eye chili, finely chopped
- 2 red bell peppers, cut into 1 inch squares
- 6 cloves garlic, finely chopped
- 2 tablespoons extra-virgin olive oil
- 1.8 pounds lean, minced beef
- 4 cans (14.1 ounces each) chopped tomatoes
- ¼ cups red wine

- tablespoons tomato puree
- tablespoons turmeric powder
- 2 tablespoons cocoa powder
- 2 tablespoons ground cumin
- Pepper to taste
- ounces canned or cooked kidney beans
- A handful fresh parsley, chopped
- A handful fresh cilantro, chopped
- cups beef stock
- ounces buckwheat groats
- Salt to taste

Directions:

1. Place a Dutch oven over medium flame. Add oil and wait for it to heat. Add onion, chilies and garlic and cook until slightly soft.

2. Stir in turmeric and cumin.

3. After about 10 – 15 seconds, stir in the beef and raise the heat to high. Cook until brown.

4. Stir in wine and deglaze the pot. Cook until wine reduces to half its original quantity.

5. Stir in bell pepper, cocoa, tomato puree, kidney beans and tomatoes and mix well.

6. Cook covered, on low heat for about an hour. Add some water if at any time you find that the mixture is very thick.

7. While the chili is simmering, follow the directions on the package and cook the buckwheat.

8. Serve chili over buckwheat.

Lamb, Butternut Squash and Date Tagine

Preparation time: 15 minutes

Cooking time: 1 hour and 30 minutes

Number of servings: 8

Ingredients:

- 4 tablespoons olive oil
- 2 inches ginger, peeled, grated
- 2 teaspoons chili flakes
- 2 sticks cinnamon
- 3.5 pounds lamb neck fillet, cut into bite size pieces
- 7 ounces medjool dates, pitted, chopped
- 2.2 pounds butternut squash, cut into ½ inch cubes
- A handful fresh cilantro, chopped + extra to serve
- 2 red onions, sliced
- 6 cloves garlic grated
- 4 teaspoons cumin seeds
- 4 teaspoons turmeric powder
- Salt to taste
- 2 cans (14 ounces each) chopped tomatoes
- 1 can water
- 2 cans (14.1 ounces each) chickpeas, drained

To serve: Use any

- Cooked buckwheat
- Couscous
- Rice
- Flatbreads

Directions:

1. Place an ovenproof pan with a fitting lid or a Dutch oven, over medium flame. Add 4 tablespoons of oil and wait for it to heat. Once oil is heated, add onion and cook covered until it softens.

2. Stir in the ginger, garlic and all the spices. Cook for a few seconds until aromatic. Add 2 - 3 tablespoons of water if the spices are getting burnt.

3. Stir in the lamb. Stir until the lamb is well coated with the spice mixture.

4. Add dates, tomatoes and water and mix well. When it comes to a boil, turn off the heat.

5. Cover the pot and shift the pan into an oven preheated to 440° F, and bake for about 80 - 90 minutes or until lamb is well-cooked. Add butternut squash and chickpeas during the last 30 minutes of cooking.

6. Add cilantro and stir.

7. Serve with any one of the serving options.

Lamb and Black Bean Chili

Preparation time: 10 minutes

Cooking time: 1 hour and 30 minutes

Number of servings: 4

Ingredients:

- ¾ pound lean ground lamb
- 1 clove garlic, minced
- ½ cup dry red wine
- 1 teaspoon ground cumin
- Salt to taste
- Hot sauce to taste (optional)
- ½ cup chopped red onion
- 1 can (14.1 ounces) whole tomatoes, with its liquid, chopped
- ½ tablespoon chili powder
- 1 teaspoon dried oregano
- 1 ½ cans (15 ounces each) black beans, drained
- ½ teaspoon sugar
- Fresh cilantro sprigs (optional)

Directions:

1. Place a Dutch oven over medium flame. Add lamb, onion and garlic and sauté until brown. Break it while you stir.
2. Remove the mixture with a slotted spoon and place on a plate lined with paper towels. Discard the fat remaining in the pan. Wipe the pot clean.
3. Place the pot over medium flame. Add tomatoes, spices, oregano and salt and stir. Heat thoroughly.
4. Lower the heat and cook covered, for an hour. Add beans and hot sauce and stir.
5. Cover and simmer for about 30 minutes.
6. Sprinkle cilantro on top and serve.

Tomato, Bacon and Arugula Quiche with Sweet Potato Crust

Preparation time: 15 minutes

Cooking time: 50 minutes

Number of servings: 8

Ingredients:

- 4 cups shredded sweet potato or yam
- Salt to taste
- 1 red onion, chopped
- 2 large handfuls baby arugula
- 12 eggs
- 2 tablespoons olive oil
- 8 slices bacon, chopped
- 16 cherry tomatoes, quartered
- 6 cloves garlic, minced
- Pepper to taste
- 1 tablespoon butter or ghee

Directions:

1. To make sweet potato crusts: You can grate the sweet potatoes on a box grater or in the food processor.
2. Squeeze excess moisture from the sweet potatoes.
3. Grease 2 pie pans (9 inches each) with some of the olive oil.
4. Add butter, pepper and salt into the bowl of sweet potatoes and mix well. Press the mixture onto the bottom and a little on the sides of the pie pan.
5. Bake the crusts in an oven preheated to 450° F, for around 20 minutes or until golden brown at the edges.
6. Remove the pie crusts from the oven.
7. Meanwhile, place a skillet over medium heat. Add bacon and cook until crisp. Remove the bacon with a slotted spoon and place on a plate lined with paper towels. Discard the fat.
8. Add remaining oil into the skillet. Once oil is heated, add onions and sauté until it turns soft.
9. Stir in tomatoes and arugula and cook until the tomatoes are slightly soft.
10. Add garlic and cook for about half a minute. Turn off the heat. Cool for a while.
11. Meanwhile, crack the eggs into a bowl. Add salt and pepper and whisk well.
12. Add the slightly cooled vegetables and bacon and stir.
13. Divide the egg mixture equally and pour over the baked sweet potato crust.
14. Place the crusts into the oven and bake until the eggs are set.
15. Let it rest for 10 minutes.
16. Cut each into 4 wedges and serve.

Lentil and Sausage Stew

Preparation time: 10 minutes

Cooking time: 45 – 50 minutes

Number of servings: 8

Ingredients:

- 2 tablespoons olive oil
- 2 red onions, finely chopped
- 2 red bell peppers, sliced
- 2 ½ cups stock
- 2 packages (14.1 ounces each) sausages
- 4 cloves garlic, crushed
- 1.1 pounds lentils, rinsed
- Salt to taste
- 1 cup red wine
- Freshly ground pepper to taste

Directions:

1. Place a large pot over medium flame. Add oil. When the oil is heated, add sausages and cook until it turns brown. Remove sausages with a slotted spoon and place on a plate.

2. Add onion, garlic and pepper into the pot and cook until slightly soft.

3. Stir in stock, wine, lentils and sausages. Let the mixture come to a boil.

4. Lower the heat and cook until lentils are soft, and sausages are well-cooked.

5. Add salt and pepper to taste.

6. Serve over rice or with crusty bread.

Chinese-Style Tofu and Pork with Bok Choy

Preparation time: 15 minutes

Cooking time: 10 – 12 minutes

Number of servings: 2

Ingredients:

- 7 ounces firm tofu, chopped into 1 ½ inch cubes
- ½ pound minced pork
- ¼ cup chicken stock
- ½ tablespoon tomato puree
- ½ tablespoon soy sauce
- 1 inch ginger, peeled, grated
- 1 small shallot, chopped
- ½ tablespoon olive oil
- 3.5 ounce Bok Choy
- ½ cup chopped parsley
- ½ tablespoon corn flour mixed with ½ tablespoon water
- ½ tablespoon rice wine
- ½ teaspoon brown sugar
- 2 small cloves garlic, peeled, crushed
- 1.75 ounces shiitake mushrooms, sliced
- 1.75 ounces beansprouts
- Salt to taste

Directions:

1. Place tofu over layers of paper towels. Place more paper towels on top of the tofu. Let it remain like this for a few minutes for the extra moisture to drain off.

2. Combine cornstarch mixture, stock, tomato puree, ginger, garlic, soy sauce, rice wine and brown sugar in a bowl.

3. Place a pan over high flame. Add oil and wait for the oil to heat. Once heated, add mushrooms and cook for a couple of minutes or until cooked. Using a slotted spoon, take out the mushrooms from the pan.

4. Add tofu into the pan and cook until golden brown all over. Take out the tofu with a slotted spoon and place on a plate.

5. Add Bok Choy and shallot into the pan and cook for a couple of minutes. Stir in the pork and cook until the meat is well-cooked.

6. Stir in bean sprouts, tofu and mushrooms and heat thoroughly.

7. Add parsley and mix well. Turn off the heat.

8. Serve hot.

Turmeric Baked Salmon

Preparation time: 10 minutes

Cooking time: 20 minutes

Number of servings: 2

Ingredients:

- 2 skinned salmon fillets
- 2 teaspoons turmeric powder
- 2 teaspoons extra-virgin olive oil
- 4.2 ounces cooked or canned green lentils
- 2 bird's eye chili's, finely chopped
- 2 teaspoons mild curry powder
- 1 cup chicken stock
- Juice of ½ lemon
- 1 medium red onion, finely chopped
- 2 cloves garlic, peeled, finely chopped
- 10.5 ounces celery, cut into 1 inch pieces
- 2 tomatoes cut into wedges
- 2 tablespoons chopped parsley

Directions:

1. Place a pan over medium-low flame. Add oil and wait for it to heat. Once oil is heated, add onion, ginger, garlic, celery and chili and stir-fry until slightly soft.

2. Stir in the curry powder. Keep stirring for a few seconds.

3. Stir in the tomatoes, lentils and stock. Let it cook for about 10 minutes. Add parsley and mix well. Turn off the heat.

4. Meanwhile, combine lemon juice, oil and turmeric powder into a bowl and brush this mixture over the salmon. Rub it into the salmon.

5. Lay the salmon on a baking dish.

6. Bake the crusts in an oven preheated to 400° F, for around 8 – 10 minutes or until cooked through.

7. Serve lentil mixture with salmon.Prawn Arrabbiata

Preparation time: 10 minutes

Cooking time: 25 – 30 minutes

Number of servings: 2

Ingredients:

- 10 ounces raw or cooked, king prawns
- 2 tablespoons extra-virgin olive oil
- 4.6 ounces buckwheat pasta

For Arrabbiata sauce:

- 1 medium red onion, finely chopped
- 1 stalk celery, finely chopped
- 2 teaspoons dried mixed herbs
- 4 tablespoons white wine (optional)
- 2 tablespoons chopped parsley
- 2 cloves garlic, peeled, finely chopped
- 2 Bird's eye chili, finely chopped
- 2 teaspoons extra-virgin olive oil + extra to drizzle
- 2 cans (14.1 ounces each) chopped tomatoes

Directions:

1. Place a skillet over medium-low flame. Add oil and wait for it to heat. Once the oil is heated, add onion, celery, garlic, dried mixed herbs and chili over medium-low flame.
2. Cook for a couple of minutes. Stir in the wine and let it cook for a couple of minutes over medium flame.
3. Lower the heat once again to medium-low and stir in the tomatoes. Cook covered for about 25 minutes, stirring occasionally.
4. Meanwhile, follow the directions on the package and cook pasta until al dente. Drain and add it back into the pot.
5. Drizzle some oil over the pasta. Toss well.
6. Add raw prawns into the sauce and stir. Simmer until they are cooked.
7. Stir in the parsley. Add cooked prawns if using, along with parsley and stir.
8. Add pasta and toss gently.
9. Serve hot.

Asian King Prawn Stir-Fry with Buckwheat Noodles

Preparation time: 10 minutes

Cooking time: 45 minutes

Number of servings: 4

Ingredients:

- 21 ounces shelled, raw king prawns, deveined
- 8 teaspoons extra-virgin olive oil
- 4 bird's eye chili, finely chopped
- 2 medium red onions, thinly sliced
- 8.6 ounces green beans, chopped
- 2 cups chicken stock
- 8 teaspoons tamari or soy sauce
- 10.6 ounces buckwheat noodles
- 4 teaspoons finely chopped fresh ginger

- 4 cloves garlic, peeled, finely chopped
- 4 stalks celery, thinly sliced
- 7 ounces kale, discard hard stems and ribs, chop the leaves
- 2 handfuls lovage, chopped

Directions:

1. Place a large pan over high heat. Add 2 teaspoons oil, tamari and prawns. Stir- fry for about 3 minutes.

2. Remove prawns from the pan and place on a plate. Clean the pan with paper towels. Place the pan back over medium-high heat. Add remaining oil and allow it to heat.

3. To cook noodles: Follow the directions on the package and cook the noodles.

4. Add garlic, ginger, celery, chili, celery, beans and kale into the pan. Stir-fry for a couple of minutes.

5. Stir in the stock. Cook until the vegetables have a crunch in them.

6. Stir in the prawns, lovage leaves and noodles.

7. When it begins to boil, turn off the heat.

8. Serve in bowls.

Walnut and Dijon Crusted Halibut

Preparation time: 15 minutes

Cooking time: 20 minutes

Number of servings: 2

Ingredients:

- ¼ cup crushed walnuts
- 1 tablespoon all-purpose flour
- 1 small egg, lightly beaten
- Salt to taste
- 2 teaspoons olive oil
- 1 tablespoon chopped fresh thyme
- ½ tablespoon Dijon mustard
- 2 halibut fillets (6 ounces each
- Pepper to taste

- Lemon wedges to serve

Directions:

1. Add walnuts and thyme into a shallow bowl and stir. Add flour into another bowl.
2. Add Dijon mustard, egg into a 3rd bowl and whisk well.
3. Sprinkle flour on the top side of the fillets. Dunk the floured part of the fillets in egg mixture. Drip off the extra egg. Season with salt and pepper.
4. Dredge this side in walnut mixture.
5. Place an ovenproof skillet over medium flame. Add oil and wait for it to heat.
6. Once oil is heated, lay the fillets in the pan, the walnut side touching the bottom of the skillet.
7. When the walnuts turn golden brown, flip sides over. Turn off the heat.
8. Shift the skillet into an oven preheated to 400° F, for around 5 - 6 minutes or until cooked through and flakes when pierced with a fork.
9. Serve walnut crusted halibut with lemon wedges.

Greek Salmon

Preparation time: 30 minutes

Cooking time: 20 minutes

Number of servings: 4

Ingredients:

For topping:

- 2 tablespoons extra-virgin olive oil
- 2 small cloves garlic, peeled, minced
- ¼ teaspoon red pepper flakes
- ½ cup cubed feta
- 2 tablespoons sliced kalamata olives
- 1 small red onion, chopped

- Juice of a lemon
- ½ teaspoon dried oregano
- Freshly ground pepper to taste
- ½ cup halved cherry tomatoes
- 2 tablespoons chopped Persian cucumber
- 1 tablespoon chopped, fresh dill

For salmon:

- ½ lemon, cut into thin round slices
- 2 salmon fillets, pat dried
- Freshly ground pepper to taste
- ½ small red onion, sliced
- Salt to taste

Directions:

1. Add oil, garlic, lemon juice, red pepper flakes, pepper and oregano into a bowl and whisk well.
2. Stir in the feta. Cover and chill for 10 minutes.
3. For salmon: Take a baking dish and lay the lemon slices and onion slices in the dish.
4. Place the salmon in the dish, with the skin side on the onion and lemon slices.
5. Sprinkle salt and pepper over the salmon.
6. Bake in an oven preheated to 375° F, for around 18 - 20 minutes or until cooked through and flakes when pierced with a fork.
7. To make topping: Add all the vegetables and dill into the bowl of feta and stir lightly.
8. To assemble: Place salmon over onion and lemon slices on individual serving plates. Scatter the topping over the salmon and serve.

Fresh Saag Paneer

Preparation time: 10 minutes

Cooking time: 20 minutes

Number of servings: 4

Ingredients:

- 4 teaspoons olive oil
- Salt to taste
- 2 inches fresh ginger, peeled, cut into matchsticks
- 2 green chilies, deseeded, finely sliced
- 14.1 ounces paneer (cottage cheese), cut into 1 inch cubes
- 2 red onions, chopped
- 2 cloves garlic, peeled, thinly sliced
- 4 tomatoes, chopped
- Freshly ground pepper to taste
- 1 teaspoon ground coriander
- ½ teaspoon turmeric powder
- 1 teaspoon salt or to taste
- 1 teaspoon ground cumin
- 1 teaspoon mild chili powder
- 1 large bunch spinach, chopped
- A large handful fresh cilantro, chopped
- A large handful fresh parsley, chopped

Directions:

1. Place a large pan with a fitting lid over high flame. Add oil and wait for it to heat.

2. Sprinkle salt and pepper over the paneer (you can use tofu instead of paneer) and add into the pan. Cook in batches if required.

3. Cook until golden brown all over. Stir frequently. Using a slotted spoon, remove the paneer and place on a plate lined with paper towels.

4. Lower the heat to medium and cook the onions in the same pan, until soft. Stir in garlic, ginger and chili. Cook for about a minute, until you get a nice aroma.

5. Stir in the tomatoes. Cover the pan and cook on low heat, for another 5 minutes.

6. Stir in all the spices and cook for a few seconds until you get a nice aroma. Do not burn the spices.

7. Add all the greens into the pan (spinach, cilantro and parsley) and mix well. Cook covered for about 5 - 6 minutes until the greens wilt. Turn off the heat.

8. Blend with an immersion blender until smooth. This step is optional.

9. Add the paneer into the pan and heat thoroughly. Taste and add salt if necessary.

10. Serve over rice or quinoa or with chapatti (a flat bread).

Asian Hot Pot

Preparation time: 15 minutes

Cooking time: 15 - 18 minutes

Number of servings: 4

Ingredients:

- 2 teaspoons tomato puree
- A large handful cilantro with stalks, finely chopped, keep the stalks separate
- A large handful parsley with stalks, finely chopped, keep the stalks separate
- 4 cups chicken stock
- 1 cup broccoli florets
- 7 ounces raw tiger prawns
- 3.5 ounces rice noodles
- 1.4 ounces sushi ginger, chopped
- 2 star anise, crushed
- Juice of a lime

- 1 carrot, cut into matchsticks
- 3.5 ounces beansprouts
- 7 ounces firm tofu, chopped
- 3.5 ounces cooked water chestnuts, drained
- 2 tablespoons miso paste

Directions:

1. Add stock, tomato puree, lime juice, star anise and the cilantro and parsley stalks into a large pan.

2. Place the pan over medium flame. When the mixture comes to a boil, lower the heat and cook for 10 minutes.

3. Stir in vegetables, tofu, prawns, water chestnuts and noodles and stir.

4. Lower the heat. Turn off the heat once prawns are cooked.

5. Add sushi ginger and miso paste and stir.

6. Garnish with parsley and cilantro leaves and serve.

Quinoa Kale Pesto Bowl with Poached Eggs

Preparation time: 15 minutes

Cooking time: 20 – 25 minutes

Number of servings: 2

Ingredients:

For kale pesto:

- ½ bunch kale, discard stems and hard ribs, torn
- 3 tablespoons walnuts
- 1 tablespoon grated parmesan cheese
- 1 ½ tablespoons extra-virgin olive oil
- 2 small cloves garlic, peeled
- 1 tablespoon lemon juice
- 1 tablespoon grated Romano cheese
- 2 tablespoons water or more if required

For quinoa bowl:

- ½ cup quinoa, rinsed
- Zest of ½ lemon, grated
- 2 eggs
- 2 teaspoons chopped parsley
- 1 tablespoon lemon juice
- 1 tablespoon chopped walnuts
- Red pepper flakes to taste
- Salt to taste
- ½ tablespoon olive oil

Directions:

1. To make kale pesto: Blanch kale in a pot of boiling water for 3 minutes with salt and garlic added to it. Remove with tongs and place in a colander. When cool enough to handle, press some of the liquid from the kale.

2. Place kale, walnuts, lemon juice and garlic into a blender and blend until coarse in texture. Add parmesan, red pepper flakes, parmesan and Romano cheese and blend until well combined.

3. With the food processor running, pour water through the feeder tube until the desired consistency is reached – creamy is preferred.

4. Pour into a bowl and add olive oil. Stir until well combined.

5. Place a pan over medium-high flame. Add oil. When the oil is heated, add quinoa and stir-fry for a minute or until dry.

6. Pour water and salt to taste and mix well. When it comes to a boil, reduce the heat to low heat and cook covered until dry. Turn off the heat and let it sit covered for about 5 minutes.

7. Uncover and loosen the quinoa with a fork.

8. While the quinoa is cooling, poach the eggs. You can use the kale cooked water for poaching the eggs.

9. Add salt, pepper, lemon juice and kale pesto to taste and stir.

10. Serve quinoa in bowls garnished with lemon zest, red pepper flakes and walnuts and topped with egg.

Braised Puy Lentils

Preparation time: 10 minutes

Cooking time: 1 hour and 30 minutes

Number of servings: 2

Ingredients:

- 16 cherry tomatoes, halved
- 3 ounces red onion, thinly sliced
- 2 stalks celery, thinly sliced
- 2 cloves garlic, finely chopped
- 1 medium carrot, peeled, thinly sliced
- 2 teaspoons dried thyme
- 2 teaspoons paprika
- 4 teaspoons extra-virgin olive oil
- 2 cups vegetable stock
- 5.3 ounces puy lentils, rinsed
- 3.5 ounces kale, chopped
- A large handful arugula
- 2 tablespoons chopped parsley

Directions:

1. Spread the tomatoes in a baking pan.
2. Bake in an oven preheated to 250° F, for about 30-35 minutes.
3. Place a saucepan over medium-low heat. Add 2 teaspoons olive oil and wait for the oil to heat. Once the oil is heated, add onion, celery, garlic and carrot and sauté for a couple of minutes.
4. Add thyme and paprika and mix well. Cook for 40 – 50 seconds until fragrant.
5. Add lentils and stock. When it comes to a boil, lower the heat and cook covered until soft. Stir often. Add some water if you find that the liquid in the saucepan is drying.
6. Stir in the kale and cook until kale wilts. Add parsley and tomatoes and mix well.

7. Serve arugula on 2 individual serving plates. Trickle a teaspoon of oil on each plate and serve with puy lentils.

Baked Potatoes with Spicy Chickpea Stew

Preparation time: 10 minutes

Cooking time: 60 minutes

Number of servings: 2 – 3

Ingredients:

- 2 – 3 baking potatoes
- red onion, finely chopped
- ½ inch fresh ginger, peeled, grated
- tablespoon cumin seeds
- Water, as required
- tablespoon unsweetened cocoa powder
- yellow bell pepper, cut into 1 inch square pieces
- Salt to taste
- tablespoon olive oil
- Pepper to taste
- cloves garlic, peeled, grated
- teaspoon red chili flakes or to taste
- tablespoon turmeric powder
- can (14.1 ounces) chopped tomatoes
- can (14.1 ounces) chickpeas with its liquid
- tablespoon chopped parsley + extra to garnish

Directions:

1 Prick the potatoes all over, with a fork. Place potatoes on a baking sheet.

2 Roast the potatoes in an oven preheated to 400° F for about 50 – 60 minutes or until cooked through.

3 To make chickpea stew: Place a soup pot over medium flame. Add oil. When the oil is heated, add cumin. When cumin crackles, add onion and cook until translucent.

4 Stir in ginger, garlic and chili. Lower the heat and cook for a couple of minutes, until fragrant.

5 Stir in turmeric. Add a couple of tablespoons of water if required.

6 Add tomatoes, chickpeas, bell pepper, cocoa, salt, pepper and parsley and mix well. Cover and cook for about 30 minutes.

7 Serve over baked potatoes.

Kale and Red Onion Dhal with Buckwheat

Preparation time: 10 minutes

Cooking time: 30 minutes

Number of servings: 8

Ingredients:

- 3 ounces red lentils, rinsed
- 2 tablespoons olive oil or butter or ghee
- ½ teaspoon minced garlic
- 1 teaspoon finely chopped fresh ginger
- Salt to taste
- ½ cup water
- ½ small red onion, finely chopped
- ½ bird's eye chili, sliced
- 1 teaspoon turmeric powder
- 1 teaspoon garam masala
- 1 cup coconut milk
- A handful kale
- Cooked buckwheat groats or brown rice to serve

Directions:

Place a pan over medium flame. Add oil. When the oil is heated, add onion and cook until translucent. Stir in ginger, garlic and bird's eye chili and stir for a few seconds until aromatic.

Stir in garam masala and turmeric. Sprinkle some water and stir for a minute.

Stir in the lentils, water and coconut milk. Cook covered until tender. Add more water if the lentils are not cooked and there is no liquid left in the pan. The cooked dhal should be of free flowing consistency.

Add salt and taste. Stir in kale and cover the pan. Simmer for a few more minutes.

Serve over hot cooked rice or with chapatti's (a type of flat bread).

Tuscan Bean Stew

Preparation time: 15 minutes

Cooking time: 30 – 40 minutes

Number of servings: 8

Ingredients:

- 4 tablespoons extra-virgin olive oil
- 1 large carrot, peeled, finely chopped
- 4 cloves garlic, finely chopped
- 4 teaspoons herbes de Provence
- 4 cans (14.1 ounces each) chopped Italian tomatoes
- 2 cans (14.1 ounces) mixed beans
- 4 tablespoons chopped parsley
- Pepper to taste
- 1 medium red onion, finely chopped
- Salt to taste
- 2 stalks celery, finely chopped
- 2 bird's eye chili's, finely chopped
- 4 cups vegetable stock
- 4 teaspoons tomato puree
- 10 large kale leaves, discard hard stem and ribs, chopped
- 5.6 ounces buckwheat groats

Directions:

Place a Dutch oven or a heavy pot over medium flame. Add oil and let it heat. When the oil is heated, add onion, celery, chili, carrot, garlic and herbes de Provence and mix well.

Cook for 3 - 4 minutes.

Stir in stock, tomato puree and tomatoes. When it begins to boil, add beans and cook for 25 - 30 minutes.

Stir in the kale and cook until kale wilts. Stir in the parsley and bird's eye chili.

To cook buckwheat: follow the directions on the package and cook the buckwheat. Make the buckwheat 15 minutes before serving.

Serve stew over buckwheat.

Wine & Grilled Cheese

Preparation time: 15 minutes

Cooking time: 10 - 12 minutes

Number of servings: 2

Ingredients:

- 4 slices French bread
- 1 red onion, chopped
- ¼ teaspoon dried thyme
- 6 tablespoons red wine
- 2 - 4 tablespoons butter
- 2 cloves garlic, peeled, minced
- 2 tablespoons flour
- 1 cup shredded gruyere cheese

Directions:

1 Place a pan over medium flame. Add butter and wait for it to melt. Stir in the onion and cook until slightly soft.

2 Stir in garlic and dried herbs and cook for about a minute.

3 Add flour and stir until well combined. Pour wine and stir constantly until the mixture is thick and the wine has dried off. It should be thick enough to coat the back of a spoon.

4 Turn off the heat and spread the mixture on one side of each slice of bread.

5 Spread cheese on 2 of the bread slices. Cover with the remaining slices of bread, with the sauce side facing down.

6 Apply butter on the outer sides of the sandwich.

7 Place a grill pan over medium flame. Place the sandwiches in the pan and cook until the bottom side is golden brown.

8 Turn the sandwich over and cook the other side until golden brown.

9 Cut into desired shape and serve.

Red Wine Roasted Mushrooms on Goat Cheese Garlic Toasts

Preparation time: 12 minutes

Cooking time: 25 – 30 minutes

Number of servings: 2

Ingredients:

- 6 ounces mini mushrooms
- 1 tablespoon unsalted butter, melted
- 1 clove garlic, minced
- 1 tablespoon finely chopped oregano
- 1 tablespoon fresh, chopped parsley
- 1 teaspoon fresh chopped thyme
- Pepper to taste
- 2 tablespoons unsalted butter, at room temperature
- 6 ounces goat cheese, at room temperature
- ¼ cup red wine
- 1 tablespoon olive oil
- Salt to taste

- ½ loaf artisan grain bread, sliced
- ¼ teaspoon garlic salt

Directions:

1 Combine mushrooms, butter, oil, garlic, oregano and thyme in a bowl.

2 Stir in the wine.

3 Roast the mushrooms in an oven preheated to 425° F, for about 30 minutes or until mushrooms are tender. Stir a couple of times while baking.

4 Add salt, pepper and parsley and toss well.

5 Butter the bread slices and place them on a baking sheet. Place it in the oven and bake to the desired crispiness.

6 Take out the bread slices and cool for 3 to 4 minutes.

7 Apply goat cheese on one side of the bread slices. Spread mushrooms over the bread slices and serve.

Kale & Garlic Frittata

Preparation time: 10 minutes

Cooking time: 20 minutes

Number of servings: 3

Ingredients:

- 2 leaves kale, chopped
- 1 small red onion, diced
- Pepper to taste
- 3 large eggs
- 1 tablespoon butter
- 1 clove garlic, minced
- ½ teaspoon paprika
- Salt to taste

Directions:

1 Prepare a small baking dish by greasing it with some cooking spray.

2 Steam kale in the steaming equipment you have. Set aside to cool for a few minutes.

3 Place a pan over medium flame. Add butter. When butter melts, add onions and cook until tender. Stir in salt, pepper, paprika and garlic and cook for a couple of minutes. Turn off the heat and transfer into the baking dish. Also add kale and mix well.

4 Whisk eggs in a bowl along with salt and pepper. Pour into the baking dish, over the kale mixture.

5 Bake the frittata in an oven preheated to 350° F, for about 10 minutes or until the eggs are set.

Chapter 10: Desserts

Chocolate Cupcakes with Matcha Icing

Preparation time: 15 minutes

Cooking time: 18 minutes

Number of servings: 24

Ingredients:

For dry ingredients:

- 10.5 ounces self-rising flour
- 4.2 ounces cocoa
- 1 teaspoon fine espresso coffee
- 14.1 ounces caster sugar
- 1 teaspoon salt

For wet ingredients:

- 1 teaspoon vanilla extract
- 2 eggs
- 1 cup milk
- 3.4 ounces vegetable oil
- 1 cup boiling water

For icing:

- 3.5 ounces butter, at room temperature
- 2 tablespoons matcha green tea powder
- 3.5 ounces cream cheese, softened
- 3.5 ounces icing sugar
- 1 teaspoon vanilla bean paste

Directions:

1 Prepare a cupcake tin by lining 24 of the wells with disposable paper liners.

2 Combine all the dry ingredients in a bowl i.e. flour, cocoa, espresso, sugar and salt.

3 Add milk, eggs, oil and vanilla. Whisk well.

4 Pour the mixture of wet ingredients into the bowl of dry ingredients and beat with an electric hand mixer until well incorporated.

5 Add boiling water gradually, beating simultaneously on low. Beat until well incorporated.

6 Now beat on high speed for about a minute to make the batter airy. The batter will be slightly runny.

7 Pour batter into the prepared cupcake tin.

8 Bake the cupcakes in an oven preheated to 350° F, for about 15 - 18 minutes. When the cupcakes are ready, if you press the top of the cupcake, it should spring back.

9 Cool the cupcakes on your countertop.

10 Meanwhile, make the icing: Combine butter and icing sugar in a bowl and beat until creamy.

11 Beat in vanilla and matcha. Beat in the cream cheese.

12 Transfer the icing into an icing bag and pipe the icing onto the cakes.

Healthy Matcha Cake with Matcha Frosting

Preparation time: 20 minutes

Cooking time: 30 – 40 minutes

Number of servings: 15 – 18

Ingredients:

For cake:

- 4 cups whole-wheat pastry flour
- 1 teaspoon baking soda
- 3 teaspoons double-acting baking powder
- ½ cup arrowroot starch
- ½ teaspoon salt
- 8 large eggs
- 2 tablespoons vanilla extract
- 2 teaspoon almond extract
- 2/3 cup vanilla whey protein powder
- 1 cup plain, nonfat Greek yogurt
- 1 ½ cups unsweetened applesauce
- 4 teaspoons liquid stevia
- 1 cup granulated erythritol
- 4 tablespoons matcha powder

For frosting:

- 3 cups fat-free cottage cheese
- 2 teaspoons vanilla paste
- 1 teaspoon almond extract
- 4 tablespoons matcha powder
- 8 ounces Neufchatel cream cheese, softened
- 2 teaspoons liquid stevia
- 2 cups vanilla whey protein powder

Directions:

1 To make cake: Prepare 2 large cake pans (of the same size) by spraying with cooking spray. Line it with parchment paper.

2 Add whole-wheat flour, baking powder, arrowroot, salt and baking soda into a bowl and stir well.

3 Add eggs, yogurt, applesauce, stevia, vanilla and almond extracts into another bowl and whisk until well incorporated.

4 Add protein powder, erythritol and matcha powder and continue whisking until well incorporated and free from lumps.

5 Add the flour mixture and continue whisking until just combined, making sure not to over-mix.

6 Divide the batter among the prepared baking pans.

7 Bake the cakes in an oven preheated to 325° F, for about 30 - 35 minutes or until firm on top. When the cakes are ready, if you press the top of the cupcake, it should spring back.

8 Cool the cakes on your countertop. Invert the cakes on plates and peel off the parchment paper.

9 Place one cake on a cake stand.

10 To make frosting: Add cottage cheese and cream cheese into a blender and blitz until smooth in texture. You can also blend it using an electric hand mixer.

11 Blend in the vanilla, almond extract and stevia.

12 Next goes in the protein powder and matcha powder and blitz until smooth.

13 Spread some of the frosting on the cake (the one on the cake stand). Carefully place the other cake over the frosted cake. Spread frosting on top and sides of the cake.

14 Chill for a couple of hours.

15 Slice and serve.

Buckwheat Chocolate Walnut Brownie

Preparation time: 15 minutes

Cooking time: 60 minutes

Number of servings: 12

Ingredients:

- 8.8 ounces compound dark chocolate
- 2 cups brown sugar
- ½ cup cocoa powder
- 4 eggs
- 1 cup chopped walnuts
- 5.3 ounces butter
- 1 ½ cups buckwheat flour
- 1 teaspoon baking powder
- ½ cup warm milk, if needed
- 4 tablespoons cacao nibs
- 2 teaspoons whole wheat flour

Directions:

1 Prepare a brownie pan by greasing it with oil. Line it with butter paper.

2 Add chocolate and butter into a microwave safe container and melt the mixture in a microwave. Stir every 15 seconds until it melts.

3 Add eggs into a bowl and whisk well. Whisk in sugar, ¼ cup at a time and beat well each time.

4 Pour melted chocolate and whisk until well combined.

5 Combine cocoa, baking powder and buckwheat flour in a bowl. Add the mixture of dry ingredients into the bowl of chocolate mixture, a tablespoon at a time and fold gently each time.

6 Spoon the batter into the baking pan.

7 Combine cacao nibs and walnuts in a bowl. Sprinkle wheat flour over it and toss well.

8 Scatter cacao nibs and walnut mixture over the batter and swirl lightly.

9 Bake the brownies in an oven preheated to 300° F, for about 10 minutes or until firm on top. It will be slightly sticky in the middle.

10 Cool to room temperature. Cut into 12 equal squares and serve.

11 Store leftovers in an airtight container in the refrigerator. It can last for 4 – 5 days.

Healthy Matcha Green Tea Coconut Fudge

Preparation time: 30 minutes

Cooking time: 0 minutes

Number of servings: 18

Ingredients:

- 2 cups low-fat cottage cheese, at nearly the room temperature
- ¾ teaspoon stevia extract
- 6 tablespoons powdered erythritol
- tablespoons raw coconut butter, melted
- tablespoons low-fat unsweetened shredded coconut
- ½ teaspoon vanilla paste
- tablespoon matcha powder
- tablespoon psyllium husk mixed with 1 tablespoon erythritol

Directions:

1 Prepare a large, brownie pan by lining it with parchment paper.

2 Place cottage cheese, stevia, erythritol, vanilla paste and matcha powder into the food processor bowl and process until well combined and smooth.

3 Pour coconut butter through the feeder tube, with the food processor running. Also sprinkle the psyllium husk mixture similarly. Turn off the food processor and spoon the mixture into the prepared pan. Spread it evenly.

4 Freeze for 2 hours. Cut into 18 equal slices.

5 Dredge the slices in shredded coconut and place them on a serving platter.

6 Chill for 7 - 8 hours before serving.

Vegan Buckwheat Chocolate Chip Cookies

Preparation time: 10 minutes

Cooking time: 10 minutes

Number of servings: 24

Ingredients:

- 2 cups buckwheat flour
- 2/3 cup melted coconut oil
- 2 teaspoons vanilla extract
- 1 teaspoon baking soda
- 1 cup dark chocolate chips
- 1 cup coconut sugar
- 4 tablespoons water
- 1 teaspoon fine sea salt
- 2 teaspoon apple cider vinegar

Directions:

1 Prepare 2 large baking sheets by lining it with parchment paper.

2 Combine buckwheat flour, oil, vanilla, baking soda, coconut sugar, water and salt in a bowl.

3 Add vinegar and mix well. Add chocolate chips and fold gently.

4 Divide the dough into 24 equal portions and place on the baking sheets. Leave sufficient gap between the cookies. Press lightly to flatten.

5 Bake the cookies in an oven preheated to 350° F, for about 10 minutes or until firm around the edges.

6 Let the cookies cool on the baking sheet for 10 minutes. Remove the cookies from the baking sheet and place on a wire rack to cool.

7 Once completely cooled, place the cookies in an airtight container. It can last for about 4 - 5 days.

Buckwheat Double Chocolate Cookies

Preparation time: 25 minutes

Cooking time: 10 minutes

Number of servings: 15

Ingredients:

- 3 tablespoons unsalted butter
- ¼ cup buckwheat flour
- ¼ teaspoon + 1/8 teaspoon baking powder
- ¼ cup + 1 tablespoon cane sugar
- ½ teaspoon vanilla extract
- 6 ounces bittersweet chocolate, chopped + extra to top
- 1 tablespoon tapioca flour
- 1 egg, at room temperature
- ¼ teaspoon fine sea salt
- Flaky salt to top

Directions:

1. Prepare 2 baking sheets by lining it with parchment paper.

2. Combine butter and about 4 ounces of chopped chocolate in a heavy saucepan and place the saucepan over low flame.

3. Cook until chocolate melts. Stir often. The mixture should not be very hot but just warm. Turn off the heat.

4. Add eggs, salt and sugar into the mixing bowl of the stand mixer. Fit the paddle attachment and set the speed to medium-high and whip until creamy.

5. Reduce the speed to low and add vanilla. Beat until just incorporated.

6. Add melted chocolate and beat well. Next goes in the flour and beat until well incorporated. Add remaining chopped chocolate and fold gently.

7. Let the batter sit for 10 minutes.

8. Place mounds of the batter on the prepared baking sheets. You should have 15 cookies in all, so adjust the batter accordingly. Leave sufficient gap between the cookies.

9. Press a few chocolate pieces on the cookies. Sprinkle flaky salt on the cookies.

10. Bake the cookies in an oven preheated to 350° F, for about 10 minutes or until firm around the edges.

11. Let the cookies cool on the baking sheet for 10 minutes. Remove the cookies from the baking sheet and place on a wire rack to cool.

12. Once completely cooled, place the cookies in an airtight container. It can last for about 3 days.

Healthy Matcha Green Tea Ice Cream

Preparation time: 30 minutes

Cooking time: 0 minutes

Number of servings: 6

Ingredients:

- 16 ounces plain, nonfat Greek yogurt
- ½ tablespoon vanilla extract
- ¼ teaspoon almond extract
- ½ teaspoon xanthan gum
- 8 ounces half and half
- 1 teaspoon liquid stevia

- 1 tablespoon matcha powder
- 1/8 teaspoon salt

Directions:

1 Add half and half, yogurt, stevia, vanilla and almond extracts into the mixing bowl of the stand mixer.

2 Set the mixer on low and mix until well combined.

3 Add salt, xanthan gum and matcha powder into a small bowl and whisk until well combined.

4 Raise the speed to medium and add the matcha powder mix simultaneously. Whisk until well combined.

5 Transfer the mixture into the ice cream maker. Follow the manufacturer's instructions and churn the ice cream.

6 You can serve it out of the ice cream maker if you want soft serve, else add the ice cream into a freezer safe container and freeze until firm.

Coffee Ice Cream

Preparation time: 15 minutes

Cooking time: 0 minutes

Number of servings: 3

Ingredients:

- 1 can (13.6 ounces) coconut milk, chilled
- ¾ cups strong brewed coffee, chilled
- 1 teaspoon vanilla extract
- 1/3 cup maple syrup
- ½ tablespoon instant coffee granules

Directions:

1. Open the can of coconut milk and scoop the coconut cream floating on top.

2. Add coconut cream, coffee, instant coffee, maple syrup and vanilla into a blender and blend until smooth.

3. Pour into a freezer safe container. Cover the container and freeze until semi-frozen. Whisk with an electric hand mixer until creamy.

4. Freeze until use.

Strawberry Mousse

Preparation time: 20 minutes

Cooking time: 5 minutes

Number of servings: 3

Ingredients:

- 5 ounces frozen strawberries, unsweetened, thawed
- 2 tablespoons water
- 1 ½ tablespoons granulated stevia-erythritol blend
- 1 teaspoon fresh lemon juice
- ¾ teaspoon unflavored, powdered gelatin
- ½ cup heavy whipping cream

Directions:

1. Pour water into a saucepan. Scatter gelatin over it. Let it sit for 5 minutes.

2. Meanwhile, add strawberries and lemon juice into a blender and blend until smooth.

3. When the gelatin is soaked for 5 minutes, add sweetener and place the mixture over medium flame. Stir often, until well combined and dissolves completely.

4. With the blender machine running on low speed, pour the gelatin mixture through the feeder tube. Blend until well combined.

5. Pour into a bowl and place the bowl in the refrigerator.

6. While the mixture is chilling, pour cream into another bowl and whip until soft peaks are formed.

7. Add one third of the whipped cream into the chilled mixture and fold gently.

8. Add the rest of the whipped cream and swirl the cream into the mixture for double colored mousse or mix gently into the mixture until fully incorporated.

9. Chill until use.

Dark Chocolate Mousse

Preparation time: 10 minutes

Cooking time: 0 minutes

Number of servings: 8 – 10

Ingredients:

- 2 ripe avocados, peeled, pitted, chopped
- 2 tablespoons raw honey
- 1 cup cacao powder
- ½ teaspoon bird's eye chili powder
- 2 tablespoons pure vanilla extract
- ½ cup date paste or 8 medjool dates, pitted
- 2 cups full-fat coconut milk
- 2 teaspoons instant coffee
- ½ teaspoon Himalayan pink salt

Directions:

1. Add avocados, honey, date paste and coconut milk into a blender and blend until smooth.

2. Retain a little cacao powder and add the rest into the blender. Also add coffee, bird's eye chili powder, vanilla extract and salt and blend until well combined.

3. Pour the mixture into the mixing bowl of the stand mixer. Beat on high speed until the mixture turns light and fluffy.

4. Spoon into dessert bowls. Sprinkle the retained cacao powder on top.

5. Chill for 5-6 hours and serve.

Blueberry Cobbler

Preparation time: 15 minutes

Cooking time: 45 - 60 minutes

Number of servings: 4

Ingredients:

- 10 ounces frozen blueberries
- ½ cup oat flour
- ½ teaspoon baking powder
- ¼ teaspoon ground cinnamon
- ½ cup walnuts
- 5 medjool dates
- ½ teaspoon vanilla extract
- 1 cup unsweetened almond milk or coconut milk

Directions:

1. Add walnuts into a blender and blend until powdered.
2. Add oat flour, baking powder, cinnamon, almond milk, dates and vanilla and blend until smooth.
3. Transfer into a small baking dish. Scatter blueberries on top.
4. Bake in an oven preheated to 350° F, for 45 - 60 minutes.

Spiced Red Wine-Poached Pears

Preparation time: 20 minutes

Cooking time: 45 minutes

Number of servings: 8

Ingredients:

- 4 cups dry red wine like merlot
- 1 cup orange juice
- 2 sticks cinnamon
- 2 strips orange zest (3 inches each)
- 4 whole cloves
- ½ cup + 2 tablespoons coconut sugar

- 8 firm ripe pears, peeled (retain the stem), cut off a thin slice from the bottom of the pear

Directions:

1. Add wine sugar, orange juice, cinnamon, coconut sugar, orange zest and cloves into a saucepan.

2. Place the saucepan over high flame. When it begins to boil, lower the heat and place the pears upright, stem on top.

3. Cover the saucepan and cook for about 20 minutes or until the pears are soft and yet firm. Turn the pears a couple of times while cooking. Turn off the heat and let it cool completely. Leave it uncovered while cooling.

4. Now cover the saucepan and place the saucepan in the refrigerator for 12 - 14 hours. Turn the pears a couple of times while chilling.

5. Take out the pears from the poached liquid and place it in a serving bowl.

6. Place the saucepan over medium - high flame and cook until the mixture is half its original quantity. It should be slightly thick, like syrup.

7. Pour syrup over the pears and serve.

Date Squares

Preparation time: 15 minutes

Cooking time: 10 - 12 minutes

Number of servings: 6 - 8

Ingredients:

For the date layer:

- 8.8 ounces dates, pitted
- 1 tablespoon lime juice
- ¼ cup orange juice
- Zest of ½ orange, grated
- ½ cup water

- ¼ teaspoon baking soda
- ¼ teaspoon vanilla powder
- 1/8 teaspoon Himalayan pink salt

For the top and bottom layers:

- 6 tablespoons coconut oil, chilled
- ½ cup unsweetened coconut flakes, toasted
- 1/8 teaspoon baking soda
- 1/8 teaspoon Himalayan pink salt
- ¾ cup blanched, sliced almonds
- 2/3 cup coconut flour
- A pinch cream of tartar

Directions

1. Prepare a small, square baking dish by lining it with parchment paper.
2. To make the date layer: Combine dates, lime juice, orange juice, orange zest, water, baking soda, vanilla and salt in a saucepan. Place the saucepan over medium flame and cook until dry.
3. Turn off the heat and cool.
4. To make the top and bottom layer: Add coconut oil, coconut flakes, baking soda, salt, almonds, coconut flour and cream of tartar into the food processor bowl.
5. Give short pulses until just combined. Transfer the mixture into a bowl and place the bowl in the refrigerator for 15 minutes.
6. Add half the top and bottom layer mixture into the prepared baking dish. Spread it evenly and press it well.
7. Bake in an oven preheated to 350° F, for about 10 minutes, until light golden brown in color.
8. Spread the date mixture over the baked crust.
9. Scatter remaining top and bottom layer mixture over the date layer.
10. Bake a little longer until the top is golden brown in color.
11. Cool to room temperature. Cut into squares and serve.

Strawberry Rhubarb Crunch

Preparation time: 20 minutes

Cooking time: 40 minutes

Number of servings: 12

Ingredients:

- 20 stalks rhubarb, chopped (about 8 cups)
- 2 tablespoons honey
- 1 cup packed brown sugar
- 2 teaspoons ground cinnamon
- 4 cups chopped strawberries
- 2 cups rolled oats
- 1 cup chopped walnuts
- 8 tablespoons butter
- Juice of a lemon

Directions:

1. Add strawberries and rhubarb into a baking dish. Add lemon juice and honey and mix well.

2. Add oats, walnuts, cinnamon, brown sugar and butter into another bowl. Mix with your hands until small crumbs are formed.

3. Scatter this mixture over the strawberry layer in the baking dish.

4. Bake in an oven preheated to 350° F, for about 40 minutes, until golden brown in color.

5. Remove from the oven and cool for a while.

6. Serve warm or cool completely and serve.

SECTION THREE: Meal Planning

Chapter 11: Why Meal Planning is Important

What is Meal Planning?

If you don't want to waste your time sitting around and wondering about your next meal, start meal planning. The term meal planning is self-explanatory: you are planning each meal. There are three simple steps involved in meal planning, and they are as follows.

- Select the recipes for different meals
- Shop for the required ingredients
- Prep the ingredients

Over the weekend, spend some time making a note of all the recipes you want to cook the following week. Once the recipes are in place, check if you have all the required supplies at home. The final step is to prep some – or most – ingredients to simplify the cooking process. For instance, you can chop vegetables, prepared dressings, and marinades, make sauces, cook proteins, and so on. You need to do the basic prepping to reduce the cooking time. Imagine how simple cooking will be if you need only to toss the ingredients in a pan and voila, the meal is ready!

Benefits of Meal Planning

Perhaps the most obvious benefit of meal planning is that it saves your time and effort. If you plan all your meals over the weekend, you don't have to worry about your meals during the weekdays. It also gives you sufficient time to shop for the required groceries and do the basic meal prep.

Meal planning can also help save your money and stick to your food budget. Cooking at home is cheaper than eating takeout. Home-cooked meals are nutritious, delicious, and pocket-friendly. By using the simple recipes in this book, you can eat your way to a healthier life.

If you don't like the idea of food wastage or often struggle with leftovers, start meal planning. It helps you decide the quantities of meals you need to cook and reduce food wastage. It is also a great way to add some variety to your daily diet.

We all lead tiring and hectic lives, and decision fatigue is real. Knowingly or unknowingly, we are constantly deciding about multiple things. A simple way to reduce a few decisions you need to make about your diet is through meal prepping and planning. When you know what you will be eating for a specific meal on a given day, you don't have to worry about making additional decisions. Imagine all the time you can save when you don't have to think, "What do I eat?"

Chapter 12: Your Sirtfood Meal Plan

Now that you know what the Sirtfood diet is all about and the different phases involved, it is time to get started. Here is a sample 4-week meal plan you can use.

Sample Sirtfood Diet Meal Plan

Week One

Day 1

The green machine

Parsley juice with ginger and apple

Green juice #3

Salmon super salad

Day 2

Green juice #2

Kale and celery juice

Grape and melon juice

Broccoli, edamame and cabbage millet salad

Day 3
Green juice #1

Savory kale and tomato juice

Kale and black currant smoothie

Warm chicory salad with mushrooms

Day 4
Strawberry smoothie

Green juice #1

Spiced cauliflower couscous with chicken

Buckwheat superfood muesli

Day 5
Mixed berry smoothie

Berry and green tea smoothie

Smoked salmon omelet

Aromatic chicken breast with kale, red onion, and salsa

Day 6
Chocolate smoothie

Matcha green tea and pineapple smoothie

Tofu scramble with kale and sweet potatoes

Chicken butternut squash pasta

Day 7
Apple pie smoothie

Peach green iced tea

Green goddess scrambled eggs

Turkey steak with cauliflower couscous

Week Two

Day 1
Green juice #1

Mushroom scrambled eggs

Chicken Marsala

Veggie sandwich

Day 2
Green juice #2

Tofu scramble with kale and sweet potatoes

Salmon pasta salad with lemon and capers

Miso and sesame glazed tofu stir-fry

Day 3
Green juice #3

Blueberry banana pancakes with chunky apple compote

California kale Cobb salad

Day 4
Kale and celery juice

Strawberry chocolate chip buckwheat pancakes

Fresh fruit and kale salad

Springtime buckwheat risotto

Day 5
Parsley juice with ginger and apple

Buckwheat and eggs

Warm chicory salad with mushrooms

Kale, edamame and tofu curry

Day 6
The green machine

Date and walnut porridge

Strawberry buckwheat Tabbouleh

Aromatic chicken breast with kale, red onion, and salsa

Day 7

Savory kale and tomato juice

Green goddess scrambled eggs

Spring vegetable and cauliflower Tabbouleh

Chicken noodles

Week Three

Day 1

Kale and celery juice

Green juice #1

Savory kale and tomato juice

Kale stir-fry with crispy curried tofu

Day 2

Parsley juice with ginger and apple

Green juice #3

Grape and melon juice

Springtime buckwheat risotto

Day 3

Green juice #2

The green machine

Kale and celery juice

Turkey steak with spicy cauliflower couscous

Day 4

Savory kale and tomato juice

Green juice #3

Mushroom scrambled eggs

Sautéed turkey with tomatoes and cilantro

Day 5
The green machine

Green juice #1

Squash and kale gratin casserole

Spiced cauliflower couscous with chicken

Day 6
Parsley juice with ginger and apple

Green Juice #2

Vegetable omelet

Three-bean chili with spring pesto

Day 7
Kale and celery juice

Savory kale and tomato juice

Green goddess scrambled eggs

Ricotta sandwiches with carrot, kale, and walnut-parsley pesto

Week Four
Day 1
Green juice #1

Savory tempeh breakfast sandwich

Chicken and kale curry

Lentil and sausage stew

Day 2
Green juice #2

Smoked salmon omelet

Crispy turmeric roasted potatoes

Chinese-style tofu and pork with bok choy

Day 3
Green juice #3

Date and walnut porridge

Roast beef wrap

Turmeric baked salmon

Day 4
Kale and celery juice

Blueberry banana pancakes with chunky apple compote

Chickpeas, quinoa, and turmeric curry

Orecchiette with sausage and chicory

Day 5
The green machine

Tofu scramble with kale and sweet potatoes

Greek salmon

Steak with spicy chimichurri sauce

Day 6
Parsley juice with ginger and apple

Mushroom scrambled eggs

Walnut and Dijon crusted halibut

Sautéed turkey with tomatoes and cilantro

Day 7
Savory kale and tomato juice

Green goddess scrambled eggs

Asian king prawn stir-fry with buckwheat noodles

Kale, pumpkin seed and potato one pot dinner

Conclusion

The Sirtfood diet is steadily gaining popularity and for all the right reasons. It is based on the idea of inclusion and not exclusion, unlike other conventional diets.

This diet encourages the consumption of certain foods rich in sirtuins. From red wine to dark chocolate, there are different superfoods you will consume. Sirtuins are a group of proteins that regulate the body's metabolism and speed up weight loss while improving your overall physical wellbeing. Unlike fad diets – promising amazing results but failing to a deliver – the Sirtfood diet is here to stay. Several celebrities, such as the Grammy-winning singer Adele and celebrity chef Lorraine Pascal swear by this diet.

From learning how this diet functions to the different benefits it offers, to a list of sirtuin-rich foods and tips to get started, everything you need is included in this book. You were also given several Sirtfood diet recipes. With this diet, you can eat your way to better health, life, and fitness. The simple 4-week meal plan and the meal planning tips will make transitioning to the Sirtfood diet quite simple.

All the recipes in this book are easy to cook, nutritious, and absolutely delicious. You don't have to spend hours together in the kitchen to cook diet food or compromise on your taste buds. Follow the simple protocols of this diet and use the different recipes mentioned in this book. You merely need to stock up your kitchen with Sirtfood diet-friendly ingredients, pick a recipe you like, and follow the instructions. Yes, it is as simple as that!

As with any other change, you need to be patient with yourself. Stick to this diet for a couple of weeks, and you will see a positive change. Consistency, effort, patience, dedication, and self-love are important factors you cannot overlook while making a dietary change. Once your body gets used to this diet, following it becomes extremely simple. The key to your good health and fitness lies in your hands. Take control of your life today, and follow the Sirtfood diet immediately.

Thank you, and all the best!

Resources

https://www.healthline.com/nutrition/Sirtfood-diet#section3

https://www.thekitchn.com/wait-what-exactly-is-meal-planning-241617

https://www.marieclaire.co.uk/life/health-fitness/the-Sirtfood-diet-22576

References

5 Emerging Benefits and Uses of Chicory Root Fiber. (2019, November 14). Healthline. https://www.healthline.com/nutrition/chicory-root-fiber#1.-Packed-with-the-prebiotic-fiber-inulin

9 Benefits of Arugula. (2014, June 30). EcoWatch. https://www.ecowatch.com/9-benefits-of-arugula-1881929191.html

15 Best Fat Burning HIIT Workouts: Exercise Plan For Women. (2017, November 29). STYLECRAZE. https://www.stylecraze.com/articles/hiit-exercises-to-burn-fat/

Admin. (2016, January 21). *The Sirtfood Diet Asian king prawn stir-fry with buckwheat noodles.* Red Online. https://www.redonline.co.uk/food/recipes/a521490/how-to-make-sirts-asian-king-prawn-stir-fry-buckwheat-noodles/

admin. (2019, July 2). *Sirtfood Diet And Exercise.* SIRTFOOD DIET. https://sirtfooddiet.net/articles/sirtfood-diet-exercise/

Articles. (n.d.). SIRTFOOD DIET. Retrieved from https://sirtfooddiet.net/articles

Beauty, Fashion, Recipes & Entertaining ideas for smart, confident women - Red magazine. (n.d.). Red Online. Retrieved from https://www.redonline.co.uk/

BENEFITS OF EATING DATES. (n.d.). Retrieved from https://carolineschoice.com/benefits-of-eating-dates/

Can birds eye chili help in weight loss? What's the benefit of taking birds eye chilies in your diet? (2020, September 1). Healthyliving from Nature - Buy

Online. https://healthyliving.natureloc.com/can-birds-eye-chili-help-in-weight-loss-whats-the-benefit-of-taking-birds-eye-chilies-in-your-diet

Did "The Sirtfood Diet" help Adele lose weight? Here is what to know about it. (n.d.). TODAY.com. Retrieved from https://www.today.com/health/what-sirtfood-diet-adele-s-rumored-diet-explained-t181146

Guarente, L. (2007). Sirtuins in Aging and Disease. *Cold Spring Harbor Symposia on Quantitative Biology, 72*(1), 483–488. http://symposium.cshlp.org/content/72/483

Hali Bey Ramdene. (2017, March 19). *The Beginner's Guide to Meal Planning: What to Know, How to Succeed, and What to Skip.* Kitchn; Apartment Therapy, LLC. https://www.thekitchn.com/the-beginners-guide-to-meal-planning-what-to-know-how-to-succeed-and-what-to-skip-242413

Harris, S. (2020, June 11). *Weight loss: How matcha green tea helps burn fat - the drink behind Adele's weight loss.* Express.co.uk. https://www.express.co.uk/life-style/diets/1294240/weight-loss-matcha-green-tea-burn-fat-superfood-adele

Healthline: Medical information and health advice you can trust. (2019). Healthline.com. https://www.healthline.com

How These Little Known Proteins Impact Healthy Aging | Thorne. (n.d.). Www.Thorne.com. Retrieved from https://www.thorne.com/take-5-daily/article/how-this-little-known-enzyme-impacts-healthy-aging

Kale and Red Onion Dhal with Buckwheat (Vegan). (2016, July 14). Easy Peasy Foodie. https://www.easypeasyfoodie.com/kale-red-onion-dhal-buckwheat/#wprm-recipe-container-8600

Recipes Archive. (n.d.). The Sirtfood Diet. Retrieved from http://www.thesirtfooddiet.com/recipes/

SirtFood Breakfast Scramble - Learning Patience. (n.d.). Www.Thehinzadventures.com. Retrieved from https://www.thehinzadventures.com/2016/03/18/sirtfood-scramble-eggs/

Sirtfood Chicken & Kale Curry | RoseFit Personal Trainer. (n.d.). Retrieved from http://www.rosefit.co.uk/recipe/sirtfood-chicken-kale-curry/

Stacey, S. (2016, February 14). *HEALTH: Love your lovage!* Mail Online. https://www.dailymail.co.uk/home/you/article-3438627/HEALTH-Love-lovage.html

The Benefits of Red Wine for Health, Skin and Weight Loss. (n.d.). Femina.In. Retrieved from https://www.femina.in/wellness/health/the-benefits-of-red-wine-for-health-skin-and-weight-loss-137432.html

The Sirt Diet Explained. (2016, February 10). HelloFresh Food Blog. https://blog.hellofresh.co.uk/sirt-diet-foods-sirtuins/

The Sirtfood Shopping List. (n.d.). Doctoroz.com. Retrieved from https://www.doctoroz.com/gallery/sirtfood-shopping-list?gallery=true&page=10

Weight Loss: Hence Proved! Coffee Can Help You Lose Weight. (n.d.). NDTV.com. Retrieved from https://www.ndtv.com/health/weight-loss-hence-proved-coffee-can-help-you-lose-weight-heres-everything-you-need-to-know-2059049

Yoga for Weight Loss: 9 Asanas to Help You Lose Weight. (2019, August 21). HealthifyMe Blog. https://www.healthifyme.com/blog/yoga-weight-loss-9-asanas/

www.ingramcontent.com/pod-product-compliance
Lightning Source LLC
Chambersburg PA
CBHW050509240426
43673CB00004B/158